PRAISE FOR *QUIT BEING SO GOOD*

"If it's moxie you're looking for, Kristi Hemmer's new book has plenty of it! With humor, candor, and a distinctive approach, Hemmer provides suggestions for how you can get your needs met directly and unapologetically. Not for the faint of heart, but rather for women ready to break out of their self-imposed constraints with abandon and gusto."

—**Lois P. Frankel**, PhD, author of
Nice Girls Don't Get the Corner Office

"In *Quit Being So Good*, Kristi Hemmer mixes stories from her childhood, and from her grown-up travels and work all over the world to show girls and women they can find the deepest fulfillment from growing to become more of themselves, not shrinking to be less of who they are. She illustrates that thriving in life is a goal that can take as many forms for women and girls as it can for men and boys, even when it means that girls and women defy expectations of how they 'should' act or exist in this world. This book is like a series of long talks with your best girlfriend, aunt, or mentor. It leaves you inspired, resolved, and ready to use your power for good in your own life and in the lives of others."

—**Emily Yellin**, journalist and author of *Our Mothers' War*

"Hemmer's personal anecdotes and expansive life view provide a courageous and unapologetic roadmap for women and girls everywhere."

—**Romy Newman**, president and cofounder of Fairygodboss

"In *Quit Being So Good*, Kristi reminds readers that much of what holds women back is in our heads. Combining her own experiences with a three-step process, she encourages readers to dig deep, question everything, and use our power to topple structural inequities in our professional and personal lives."

—**Renee M. Powers**, founder and CEO of Feminist Book Club

QUIT
BEING
SO
GOOD.

STORIES OF
~~A SMART, NICE GIRL~~
AN UNAPOLOGETIC WOMAN

KRISTI HEMMER

ISBN 13: 978-1-63489-417-3

Library of Congress Catalog Number has been applied for.
Printed in the United States of America
First Printing: 2021

25 24 23 22 21   5 4 3 2 1

Cover design by Athena Currier
Interior design by Patrick Maloney

Wise Ink Creative Publishing
807 Broadway St NE
Suite 46
Minneapolis, MN 55413

To all those who have been told *Quit Being So Good*, this book is for you. Keep it up; other women and girls are watching.

Katie,

Moxiem!

♡ Kristi

TABLE OF CONTENTS

The truth will set you free, but first it will piss you off.

—GLORIA STEINEM

DUBUQUE, IOWA, JANUARY 1983.

When I was in eighth grade, my Future Problem Solvers of America team was the only one from my junior high to advance to state. It was a big deal. My mom took me to JCPenney, where I picked out a brand-new maroon corduroy blazer with puffy sleeves and new navy pants with an elastic waist to fit the belly that was getting ready for my first period. I would be the most fashionable Problem Solver out there.

Growing up, I was labeled the "smart, nice girl." I was told I was smart by teachers, my family, and my friends. As a Future Problem Solver champion, I was labeled as smart. With my Coke-bottle glasses, I looked smart.

But on this Future Problem Solver team, I was the dumbest of the smart. Everybody knew Kathy was the smartest—then Lavonne, Colleen, Lisa, and me. On competition day, we were told that only four of us could compete on the team. One of us would need to step down. I volunteered right away; I felt it was the smart and nice thing to do.

Curious, I recently looked on the Future Problem Solving Program's website from the year I competed and noted the problems that needed to be solved in 1983 were Electronic Games, Prisons, Lasers, Nuclear Waste, and Genetic Engineering.

Thinking of my "smart, nice" label, I wondered, "But what about the topic of Identity?" As an educator I saw girls shrink in eighth grade and the boys take up even more space. And when I was an eighth grader, I started to shrink and drop out of things I liked and was good at—like the Future Problem Solver Team.

As an educator and counselor, I knew from Joan and Erik Erikson's stages of psychosocial development that "Identity v. Confusion" is the stage adolescents must resolve to develop a sense of self. At thirteen—when developmentally I was asking myself, "Who am I?" and "What can I be?"—the world told the rose-tinted-glasses girl to accept being "Smart, Nice Kristi." This is a problem.

Today, when I work with high-potential women and ask them what they want to be known for, the two words that are most common are "nice" and "hardworking." Of course, you need to get along with others and work hard to do well, but these labels are not differentiators. They do not show your potential, your possible, or what you want. Just like being labeled "Smart, Nice Kristi" did not serve me, because I was so much more than that.

I liked to be on stage. I liked to dance. I liked winning. I liked competition. I liked writing. I liked leading. And I really liked learning.

I wanted to be a teacher when I grew up—and that's what I did. I became a teacher who was intentional about not letting society's labels define potential. A principal at an all-girls school who coached not only her girls to be self-assured—but also her all-female faculty. A counselor who "recognized the equality and full humanity" of girls and boys. What Gloria Steinem would call a feminist.

JAPAN, AUGUST 2007.

When I started teaching in 1992, I said I would never teach above second grade; my first job was teaching third grade in inner-city Houston. My principal saw my ability to bring out the best in each student, influence social consciousness, and stretch all of them into their best possible selves, and he said I was needed in middle school. I trusted his judgment and indeed fell in love with teaching and counseling middle schoolers. To me, it was the best of both worlds: the lower-school pedagogy with the upper-school ability to solve big social problems.

I taught and was a school counselor for sixth grade for eight years at three different schools when, one fateful day in August 2007, I stepped into my international, eighth-grade Language Arts classroom. I was struck by the suffocating testosterone wafting through the room; I opened the windows. These almost-men who were taller and bigger than me took up plenty of space. The girls were tentative and quiet, took seats at the back of the room, and tried their hardest to take up no space.

This wasn't like my sixth-grade classes of the past eight years, where the girls came in talking loudly and took seats in the front and the back of the room while the boys filled in the spots.

After a quick review of the syllabus, I opened my eighth-grade class with a question. I asked, "If this class was really helpful to you now and in the future, what would you learn?"

The boys raised their hands. "How to create a video that will go viral." "How to write a song that will go viral." "How to use commas correctly." "What is the meaning of life?"

The girls sat on their hands. Boy after boy shared.

This wasn't like my sixth-grade classes, where the girls' hands flew up in the air and waved all over the place trying to get my attention while the boys waited to be called on.

Straight away, I noticed the gap between the girls and the boys. However, it was my first time teaching eighth grade, so I gave more wait time, hoping that was what was needed.

Nothing from the girls. Nothing. They had given up.

"Let's hear from the girls," I said.

Nothing.

I waited. Still nothing.

Aaron, the most popular boy in class, sighed and said, "Girls, just answer. Ms. Hemmer's not going to move on until you do."

Finally, a girl raised her hand timidly; her voice was so soft we all had to lean in to hear her. She said, "I'm not sure if this is right. But I think I'd maybe want to know how to write a college essay—if that's OK."

It was so painful. And I thought, *Why do girls shrink? With their minimizing word choices, their inaudible voices, their self-doubting thoughts, and their invisible bodies?*

And then I thought back to the years when my name was "Smart, Nice Kristi."

It was then that I painfully understood that this universal shrinking of girls' voices, ideas, and existence at a time when their identities were forming was not only a problem but a crisis.

When I was eight (one year before confidence peaks for girls in America), I was the Connect Four champ; nobody wanted to play with me. The message I heard was one I'd come to hear again and again as a girl and then as a woman: *Quit Being So Good.*

As part of the Future Problem Solvers of America team mentioned above, I was told, "Don't be too smart, boys won't like you." *Quit Being So Good.*

My best guy friend in high school said, "You're too smart to be a teacher, Hemmer." *Quit Being So Good.*

My college advisor said, "Don't show your GPA because it looks like you haven't experienced failure." *Quit Being So Good.*

When I was thirty-three and the principal of an all-girls school, a city council member told me I was too young. *Quit Being So Good.*

I didn't know it then, but my first day of teaching eighth grade was when I decided to quit being part of the problem. Three years later, I quit my job, traveled the world for four years learning from changemakers while living on twenty dollars a day, and was inspired by the young women I met around the globe to start my own social business, Academy for Women's Empowerment. Because the schools I worked in for over twenty years were more concerned that you knew how to conform than they were about equality. There was no room in the curriculum for equality.

I was pissed off.

—

Now I realize the question that I have been pushing up against since I was eight is: "Why do women and girls shrink in a classroom, boardroom, and conversation?"

As a good Future Problem Solver, I still love solving problems.

This book explores, plays with, and challenges every changemaker to imagine a future world where it's safe for a woman and girl to show up not as "Smart and Nice" but as "Unapologetic." Even if it hurts somebody's feelings.

If you identify as female, the book will give you tools to be unapologetic, stories to let you know *you're not alone*, and the MOXIE to do something about it.

If you identify as male, it's like reading your sister's diary. The book is a safe space to listen and learn, so you can be a more empathetic brother, partner, father, leader, boss, colleague, and direct report. And it will (hopefully) inspire you to help create a safer and more equitable world for women and girls.

This book is NOT about changing you. It's about showing up as MORE of who you are—even at the risk of hurting somebody's feelings. It's about reclaiming the little girl inside you who climbed to the very top of the jungle gym, who tried her best to win every time, and who was proud of being a Future Problem Solver.

Go back to when you were a little girl. Before your confidence peaked (age nine) and before you started "dropping out" of sports, your passions, and your life (age fourteen). What is something you liked to do as a little girl that you "dropped out" of? This book will help you to reclaim it.

And now, what would be different if you were creating a future where girls and women were equal and safe all over the world? If you were a Future Problem Solver.

HOW TO BE A FUTURE PROBLEM SOLVER.

1. **Take up space.** Unapologetically. What are you known for? _____ Now, what do you WANT to be known for? _____ I was known as "Smart, Nice Kristi." Today, I want to be known for inspiring changemakers to be unapologetic so that they can disrupt the systems of power to create a more equitable and safer world for women and girls. Go ahead, fill in the blanks. How will you take up space, unapologetically?

2. **Be first.** There is power in going first. As girls and women, we are taught to follow. In Scooby-Doo, Daphne and Velma follow Fred into the scary swamp. Even though it's Velma who solves the problem, Scooby and Shaggy get the credit. Be the first to speak up at the meeting, to start your own business, to choose not to get married, to live overseas, to climb Kilimanjaro, to buy a house. And then show those who are watching (and believe me, people are watching) that they can be first too.

Where do you want to "go first" in your life? What will it give you?

3. Look for the helpers. Mr. Rogers said, "When I was a boy and I would see scary things in the news, my mother would say to me, 'Look for the helpers. You will always find people who are helping.'" Mr. Rogers's quote is powerful, especially for women because women are often the helpers and struggle with asking for help. I purposely did not say, "Be a helper," because you already know how to do that. Now is the time to learn to look for the helpers.

Helpers look like many things. They can be allies. They can be sponsors. They can be men. And they can be women. Helpers can live on a dollar a day or have the glass office on the top floor in a big international city. When you're out there being more of you, you are not alone. There are helpers. Surround yourself with them. What is something scary for you right now? Who are your helpers? Now, go ask for help.

GO FORTH, FUTURE PROBLEM SOLVER. TAKE UP SPACE, UNAPOLOGETICALLY. AND MOXIEon.

P.S. MOXIE. It means guts, pluck, sass, courage, and energy. I use it as an adjective, noun, and verb. When I say "MOXIEon," I mean "Be your most powerful self and change the world."

QUIT BEING SO GOOD; YOU'RE GOING TO HURT SOMEBODY'S FEELINGS.

Women are liked better when they lose.

—GLORIA STEINEM

HOUSTON, SUMMER 2019.

I was sitting in my friend's glass, top-floor corner office in downtown Houston. The one that Nice Girls Don't (Usually) Get. Jessica Lynn had just found out that she'd overachieved the company goal by billions.

"How are we going to celebrate your success?" I asked.

Jessica Lynn pooh-poohed the idea away with her hand. "That's nothing. Let's talk about you. Tell me more about your book."

"My book is an attempt to answer my big question: *Why do girls and women shrink in a classroom, boardroom, and conversation?* It's about taking up space. A call to be unapologetic instead of the expectation to be nice and not make anybody feel bad."

"Or jealous," Jessica Lynn added.

"Have you experienced this?" I asked.

She pinched her fingers together to show a little space of light beaming through and said, "I show up a little bit less in everything I do. The board meeting. The panel. The idea for our next product."

"What would be different if you closed that gap?" I pinched my fingers together and closed them with a snap. "If you weren't a little bit less?"

She sighed and leaned back in her chair. For the first time since we'd met, she didn't have a response.

"What would the world be like if we all showed up as ourselves—and not a little bit less?" I wondered.

For me, I'd be eight years old.

MRS. BERRY'S CLASS, DUBUQUE, 1979.

When I was eight, I wrote my first book, *The Funny Boy on the Block*, as part of our third-grade class project on publishing. It is about a misfit boy (Pat Funny) who does everything "wrong" but in the end is rewarded for being true to himself. It is a lesson I am still learning.

It has a pink velveteen cover made from a wallpaper sample that my teacher got for free for our class project. My mom bought me brand-new thin-tip markers for the book. I couldn't draw hands, so my characters didn't have any.

This was the year I decided I wanted to be a published author with so many books that you would need to use the card catalog to find them all, like Judy Blume. I also wanted to be president. And I wanted to start my own school.

It was also the year I learned not to be so good. Not to be me.

I held the class record for the Multiplication Mad Minute, read the most books during our read-a-thon, and was the class champ for tetherball. Nobody wanted to play with me.

Being me was too much. It was going to hurt somebody's feelings. Somebody was going to feel less than me. Somebody was going to be jealous. And most importantly, nobody was going to want to play with me.

In fourth grade, when we did our "All About Me" book, mine

looked just like everybody else's. I was a statistic. Research shows nine years is the age confidence peaks for girls in America[1]—my fourth-grade self was proof. I was already starting to shrink.

QUIT BEING SO GOOD.

Now, I realize this problem—"Why do women and girls shrink?"—is what I've been pushing up against since I held the class record for the Mad Minute. And I'm not the only one.

With every big win, executive Jessica Lynn is not celebrated but asked by her boss, "How will your success and ambition make Jenny [the only other female executive] feel?" *Quit Being So Good.*

My cousin excelled in her job, to the point that her boss joked, "You're getting so good you could have my job." The promotion went to a woman she trained. *Quit Being So Good.*

When Brenda was the top actor in her agency, she was met with physical harassment by the man who used to be the top actor. Brenda ended up in the hospital with injuries from him when he was "acting," and only after another incident was he finally fired from the agency. *Quit Being So Good.*

Even when I pitched this book to an agent, she interrupted me and said, "This just happened to me yesterday! I was told I was making the other agents look bad." *Quit Being So Good.*

When were you stopped or discouraged from being your powerful-beyond-measure self?

What is your *Quit Being So Good* story?

Next time someone tells you to *Quit Being So Good,* don't shrink. Take up space.

---

1   Always. "Always #LikeAGirl." YouTube. https://www.youtube.com/watch?v=XjJQBjWYDTs+13+c

Because when women take up more space, companies have less employee turnover, more employee satisfaction, higher innovation, better team decision-making, and improved financial performance.[2]

What if, like Jessica Lynn, you pinched your fingers, closed that gap, and showed up as good as you can be? If you quit *Quit Being So Good*, what would be different?

HOW TO QUIT *QUIT BEING SO GOOD.*

1. Take up space. Close that gap. Take up your full space: in the boardroom, at the family dining room table, and on the Zoom call. Push up against the *Quit Being So Good* messages you receive. Taking up space may sound like speaking up twice in each conference call you're on. Or speaking up when someone makes a sexist or racist comment. Or quitting the job, relationship, or organization that rewards you for being small. How will you "take up space"?

2. Be first. Don't apologize for being you. Ever. And when you hear women and girls say, "I'm sorry," stop them! In my undergrad diversity class in 1991 at the University of Northern Iowa, I learned that there is a gender difference in the meaning of *sorry*. When women say, "I'm sorry" they usually mean "I feel bad." When men say, "I'm sorry," they usually mean, "It's my fault." When I shared this at a conference, a woman popped out of her chair with excitement. "Aha! That's why when I say, 'I'm sorry,' my boyfriend says, 'It's not your fault.' I know it's not my fault. I just feel bad." I also find that women use the word "sorry" as a filler when they need a pause. Instead, stop. Breathe. How will you stop apologizing for being you?

3. Look for the helpers. Be the sponsor who notices what's

---

2 "Why Diversity and Inclusion Matter: Quick Take." https://www.catalyst.org/research/why-diversity-and-inclusion-matter/

possible and showcases those women. When Abby Wambach scores a goal, she points at the woman who made the assist. Then, she points at the woman who blocked the woman who made the assist. Then, she points to her coach, her team, and her fans. What woman will you point to today?

NOW, GO TAKE UP SPACE, UNAPOLOGETICALLY.

I MAY BE A CRUEL, HEARTLESS B*TCH, BUT I'M GOOD AT IT.

Self-esteem isn't everything; it's that there's nothing without it.

—GLORIA STEINEM

My dear friend Trudy was working on owning her power as an executive leader at her big job at a big company in a big, international city. Her big title, big pay, and big office showed she was an executive leader already. However, she didn't feel like one. She felt like the little girl who was told to sit down, shut up, and be nice.

She was dating a man who sucked the confidence right out of her. As she focused on taking up space and succeeded, she thought more and more about breaking up with him. It was at this point that he told her, "I don't like your friend Kristi."

I was excited. This was a place where my dear friend Trudy could break her cycle of being small. The place where she could take up the space she had worked hard for, that she was good at, and that her daughters needed to see.

She confided to me over wine, "I didn't want to marry Husband #2, but he asked, so what was I to say? I said yes."

I said, "Well if you don't break up with Fred, eventually he'll ask. And then he'll be Husband #3."

A Smart, Nice Girl says yes. A Cruel, Heartless B*tch speaks her mind.

———

SPRING BREAK, NEW ORLEANS, 1993.

"I may be a cruel, heartless b*tch, but I'm good at it." My friends and I were in New Orleans for spring break, and they managed without my knowing to buy a T-shirt for me with this quote on it. I placed it up to my chest and smiled. Proud. My friends knew me so well; I loved the T-shirt!

My friends didn't have the guts to wear the shirt; I wondered which one had even had the guts to buy it. "Hemmer, be nice" was code for "Shhh. Be quiet. Stay in your place. Be small." Even though they told me to stay in my place, they saw and appreciated that I was a Cruel, Heartless B*tch. A #CHB.

I asked them what inspired them to buy it for me. None of them remembered, except Sally had this feeling that it would be a good bar shirt to warn others that "Hemmer is not nice."

Not nice. Yep. I "say something" when I see something. I challenge men when they minimize or objectify women.

In the early '90s, I was a college student in the middle of the country. Although I was a feminist who didn't know I was a feminist, I knew I wasn't a b*tch.

"The trailblazing women of the 90s were excoriated by a deeply sexist society. That's why we remember them as bitches, not victims of sexism," explains Allison Yarrow in *90s Bitch: Media, Culture, and the Failed Promise of Gender Equality.*[1]

Trailblazing. That better described me than b*tch.

---

1   Yarrow, Allison. *90s Bitch: Media, Culture, and the Failed Promise of Gender Equality.* New York: *Harper Perennial, 2018.*

COLLEGE, IOWA, 1991.

As a feminist who didn't know I was a feminist, it was a confusing time for me. Feminists weren't really talked about in the late '80s and early '90s. I didn't have any friends who called themselves feminists and really wouldn't until my late twenties.

It was the time of "Push It," "Cold-Hearted Snake," and "Hammertime" (the inspiration for my nickname—Hemmertime). One Thursday night, after my friends finished watching *90210*, we snagged a booth at our favorite college dive bar. A group of wrestlers were in a booth facing us; wrestlers were a big deal in the Midwest. They were like the T-Birds in *Grease*: greasy, raunchy, good looking, and assholes.

At first I ignored them because, like the T-Birds, they were not nice. But since I didn't watch *90210*, I wasn't interested in my booth's conversation about who was cuter: Brandon or Dylan? So I paid attention to the booth next to me. The wrestlers. My friends noticed me zoning in on the booth of wrestlers. "Hemmer, be nice," they said.

I smiled my prettiest socialized-girl smile. "I am."

Then Sally asked about who they thought Dylan would date next, and they forgot about me.

I didn't have a clue what Dylan was doing, but I was interested in what the wrestlers were doing. Scott #1 and Scott #2 were leaning across the table deep in conversation; I heard the words "steroid" and "ass" and "b*tch." The other wrestlers chattered away. And then I saw him: Rick. The ultimate bully. We locked eyes. He was the leader; they all looked up to him. Like Danny Zuko. But not as cute. Or as a good of a dancer. I wondered when the day would come when we would stand off.

And then a woman walked by, Rick's eyes followed her, and his mouth opened. "Four," he said. The other wrestlers laughed. They punched each other on the shoulder, then scratched their ball sacks. A pair of women walked by. "Two. Five." Guffaws. The first woman turned around and glanced at the table. She frowned, then turned around quickly when the laughter got louder.

They were judging women's butts; they were not quiet about it. Some of the women turned around as the wrestlers shouted out a number. Even if the targets didn't know the details, they knew what was going on. I saw their faces fall when a three or four or even nine was called out. The women's conversation instantly transformed into painful grimaces complete with furrowed brows and slumped shoulders. I was fuming. It was hard enough in college as a young woman in the early '90s to get your bangs high enough, to wear a miniskirt in below-freezing weather, and to not get raped. We did not need this.

Around my booth sat Molly, Rachel, and Sally, our regular crew. Molly was my hometown girl; she got me to my core. Rachel got us into all the rugby parties. Sally was the friend who dated the meanest guys; she had the lowest self-esteem of the crew, although nobody had solid self-esteem. Except for me—and I was labeled "Cruel, Heartless B*tch."

How did I end up with all the self-esteem? If I knew this, I would be rich and famous. For me, college was a time to bust the labels of "smart" and "nice." It was a time for me to own who I was: sharp-witted and innovative and self-assured, an outspoken leader focused on being self-actualized. I heard Maslow's call: "What a [woman] can be, [she] must be." *I must make the world safe and equal for women.* Maybe it was this journey of self-actualization and purpose that built my self-esteem. Or maybe it was because when I was thirteen, by American standards of the ever-changing perfect body mold, the just-right blue eyeshadow, and the perfect smile ready to flash to hide what we really wanted to say, I was not pretty, so I had to find something else to identify me. I deeply felt the numbers Rick was giving the women.

"Ugliness" protected me from being overly objectified and sexualized. As a teacher and school counselor, I empathized with the "geeks" and "misfits," but I really worried about the "pretty girls." All their lives, they have been identified as "pretty." They didn't have the opportunity I did to be defined by other words. At my twenty-five-year class reunion, the "pretty girls" I'd grown up with were now identified by who they married. One of the "pretty girls" was now the wife of a kinda-semi-pro something. A kinda-semi-pro something whom nobody had heard of. And she was the wife of that nobody.

One thing I know for sure: luck didn't lead me to self-esteem. I don't give my power away. Hell, maybe that was it.

Anyway, I leaned in and said, "Let's start ranking men's packages as they walk by us and call out the number just loud enough for the wrestlers to hear."

"Oh, Hemmer. They already hate you. Why would you do this?" Sally asked.

"Because they're making women feel bad. They need to know how it feels to be judged by your parts. And they need to stop the bad behavior."

As an early-childhood major, I understood the theory and practice of behavioral science. I knew you couldn't control a three-year-old, but you couldn't control a twenty-one-year-old either. You had to change behaviors with positive and negative consequences. For the wrestlers, our low rating of their manhood would be a negative consequence for a behavior I wanted to stop: rating women's butts loud enough for the women to hear. The behaviors I *really* wanted them to stop was the sexual harassment, being mean, and making women feel bad. One of the Scotts walked by. I called out, "Four!" and then gave my best *I'm smiling, so it's OK* look.

Rachel laughed. Molly smiled and said, "Oh, Hemmer." Sally got up; she couldn't handle the possibility of not being liked.

Scott #2 walked by. "Three! Oh wait. Let's make that a two!"

Rachel laughed louder. Molly started enjoying herself and grinned like a Cheshire cat; there was no stopping me now.

The wrestlers were starting to catch on. I saw them motion for Rick. You could feel the testosterone when he walked around; he was quiet and scary.

As he walked by, I looked down (really at his knees, not his package) and said with Olympian authority, "Two!" By now, my friends were all in. Molly said, "Hmmm. I've heard really bad things about him. I'd say that's a deduction." She couldn't stop giggling.

We looked at each other and declared, "One!"

Rick looked at me. Looked at our booth. And kept walking. The butt scoring stopped.

Women were able to walk by again without being judged publicly. I wasn't dumb; I knew the wrestlers were still judging, but probably more about the booth next to them rather than the other women. And at least the women who were walking by were no longer harassed.

―

On this same spring break trip to New Orleans when I got my #CHB T-shirt, I was reading Gloria Steinem's *Revolution from Within* and had it sitting on the dashboard. Rachel said, "Hemmer, flip the book over. People will think we're feminists."

"Rachel," I replied, "we are becoming the men we want to marry."

"What does that mean?" she asked.

"It's Gloria's words. Read the book and find out."

From that book, I learned to stop apologizing for being me. That it was OK to be Hemmer: powerful, outspoken, empathetic, smart, and a #CHB. To become the man I was supposed to marry.

"The book is about self-esteem; you could use some," I said to Rachel. "When I'm done, you can have it."

Thank goodness for Gloria Steinem for showing me how to be a proper Cruel, Heartless B*tch.

HOW TO BE A #CHB.

1. **Take up space.** With your friends. Although Sally stepped away, I knew she still loved me and didn't want me to change. She wasn't able to handle the conflict, but she also supported me. I accepted where she was in her journey just like she accepted where I was in mine. And our booth of smiling, nonconforming women stopped the wrestlers' bad behavior, unapologetically. I may have been the leader, but as Derek Sivers says in his TED Talk "How to Start a Movement," "It's the first follower that matters the most." When Molly chimed in and Rachel laughed, I was no longer the lone #CHB, and we were a force. A force that closed the gap. They say sponsorship is the greatest equalizer; these friends proved it. Where will you lead? Who will you follow?

2. **Be first.** To be OK with conflict. Activate your moral courage and say something. I see healthy conflict as an opportunity to disrupt, change mindsets, and make the world better. We made the bar a safer place for women to be. If you're not first to say something, be the first to stand with that person. Where do you need to speak up?

3. **Look for the helpers.** Speaking up is hard. Surround yourself with people who believe you, believe in you, and stand up next to you. Changemakers are everywhere—find them. Where do your changemakers hang out?

GO AHEAD, BE A #CHB. AND BE GOOD AT IT.

WONDER WOMAN IS NOT REAL.

A pedestal is as much a prison as any small, confined space.

—GLORIA STEINEM

"What would Wonder Woman do?" is scrawled across my writing notebook in gold. I wonder, *What would Wonder Woman do right now?* Would she fight for a nonviolent world like Eve Ensler? Would she fight for respect like Alexandria Ocasio-Cortez? Would she fight for disability rights like Haben Girma?

When I hot-roller my hair and stand on stage, I am told I look like Wonder Woman.

When I started Academy for Women's Empowerment to create a more equitable and safer world for women, I was told I am noble like Wonder Woman.

I know from my boyfriend's obsession with vintage comic books that she was created by a feminist. A man. William Moulton Marston believed that women were mentally stronger than men and that the United States would one day be ruled by a matriarchy. He shared this idea with the Harvard Club in 1937.[1] In 1942, a press release about Marston read, "'Wonder Woman' was conceived by Dr. Marston to set up a standard among children

---

1   Klein, Christopher. "Wonder Woman's Surprising Origins." https://www.history.com/news/wonder-woman-origins

ʒ people of strong, free, courageous womanhood; to
e idea that women are inferior to men, and to inspire
lf-confidence and achievement in athletics, occupa-
ırofessions monopolized by men."

Fascinated and curious, I looked up the definition of Wonder
Woman online.

*Wonder Woman: 1. A woman who can be a successful wife and
have a professional career at the same time. 2. A woman of extraordinary powers.*

Hmm . . . I'm not married and don't plan on that ever changing. Where does this leave unmarried, childless women like me?

"A woman of extraordinary powers." Power—I find women
struggle with this word. When I encourage them to "Own Their
Power" in coaching or a conversation, I usually get one or more
of the following responses: (1) Confusion; she doesn't have any
idea how to own her power. (2) Fear; she is afraid of her power.
(3) Disgust; she thinks power is a dirty word.

To clarify, the power I'm referring to is Personal Power. The
power to . . . work and raise a family. The power to . . . choose if
you want children or not. The power to . . . save money to buy a
house or send your children to college.

Not Societal Power, which is the power over . . . the wife. The
power over . . . the young woman. The power over . . . the system.

Girls and women around the world are raised to give our
power away. We are raised with an external locus of control. I
learned about the locus of control reading Mary Pipher's book
Reviving Ophelia. Locus of control is a psychological concept,
developed by Julian B. Rotter, that refers to the degree to which
individuals believe they control situations, experiences, and
outcomes in their lives. That what they do matters.

For example, I was talking on the phone with Lila, who was
considering hiring me to work with her women-in-tech group.
As I was getting to know her, she told me a story about how
when she was in college, she started a company in her dorm

room and sold it for over a million dollars before graduation. She sighed. "I am lucky."

"You're a serial entrepreneur and have managed more money than most women will have access to in their lifetimes. And you're not even thirty. That doesn't sound like luck to me," I pointed out.

"You're right. When my friends were out partying all night, I was pulling all-nighters creating presentations for men who would ignore me or hit on me. When my friends were going on spring break, I stayed on campus to finish one more proposal. When my friends were napping during their lunch breaks, I was running a business. It's grit, not luck!"

Initially, Lila was externalizing her power: luck. Then when she reflected, she internalized her power: she worked hard, sacrificed, navigated politics, and earned over a million dollars with her extraordinary powers.

Then she asked, "So how do you help women?"

I paused. "Just like I did with you. I help them see how their limiting beliefs get in the way of owning their power and taking up space. Once they own their power, they can make more space for other women."

"Let's find a date for you to come and work with us," Lila said.

EXTRAORDINARY POWERS.

When I think of "extraordinary powers," I think of my dear friend Gina, who is a "Faster than a speeding bullet! More powerful than a locomotive! And able to leap tall building in a single bound" person. She threw a going-away party for me when I moved overseas, drove on icy roads to be with me when my dad was in the hospital, and brought me SnackWell's cookies in graduate school (so I wouldn't eat all of hers). Gina can do anything and everything at the same time. From the outside it looked like

Gina had Extraordinary Powers because she was "doing it all," a real-life Wonder Woman. There was a meme going around on Facebook about checking in on your strong friends. I checked on Gina. Her brother was supposed to visit her mom before she died. I texted her, "Did your brother make it?"

"He just landed. Jeffrey [her husband] had to pick my brother up because I'm in the ER."

She sent me a photo of some growth on her leg. *Did she catch what her mom had? Is she going to lose her leg?*

"Wthuh?" I texted back.

"Bad accident in the kitchen with boiling water. I'd rather have a baby; it hurts really bad. Like I needed more adventure in my life," she replied.

I was about to text back but called instead, like the olden days before texting; I didn't want her to hide behind texts. We talked and laughed as the morphine settled in. We hugged each other over the phone line and then hung up.

My boyfriend asked, "How can you laugh when she has second-degree burns?"

That's what Wonder Woman does. But Wonder Woman isn't real.

What if he was right? How could we laugh? If we weren't laughing, we would have been crying. And we'd both been taught that crying is not OK.

DEPRESSION IS REAL.

It was August 2018. My boyfriend showed me a photo from our recent Fourth of July cabin trip with his family. I saw me. But it was not me. My eyes were empty. I was disheveled. I teared up. "Why didn't you say something?"

He was quiet. "I didn't know what to say."

This was not supposed to happen to me. I was Wonder

Woman. Business was growing. My tennis serve was improving. I was in a golf league. The POWERcamp had turned into the Academy for Girls' Empowerment and was now a national initiative in El Salvador. Women who graduated from my programs had changed policies, fought for equal pay, started employee resource groups, and challenged the status quo and were now the managers sponsoring the next round of women leaders. Thousands of lives have been changed because of my hard work and MOXIE.

And yet I was depressed. That holiday weekend, I stayed in my room and read two books. Nobody came for me. Nobody checked in on me.

I felt so alone. Alone in my failures: a big corporate deal had fallen through after it was signed, leaving me without income for three months. One of my favorite family members was struggling again with addiction. I'd gained seven pounds. I not only *felt* alone, I *was* alone. I felt nobody could handle what I was feeling. I was depressed, and nobody knew.

I'd been depressed one other time in my life. It was 1996. I knew I was depressed because I'd given my Alanis Morissette ticket away. It was a time where I was disconnected from the family system I grew up in. Giving my Alanis ticket away sounded an alarm to my friends; they knew I was not well. They stopped by my apartment randomly to check on me. Even friends of friends stopped by. They were on Kristi Watch. Back then, I created a safe space to heal and learned to lean on friends.

But this time, there was nobody on Kristi Watch. Being an entrepreneur is lonely and hard. Like having a baby, except a business is not adorable. Nobody gets mad when you spend time and energy on a new baby, but they do when it's a business. My friends and family said, "Your niece misses you." "Of course you can't talk, because you're busy." "When are you going to settle down?" Nobody noticed. I was invisible, like Wonder Woman's jet.

A month later, I visited an old friend from my Leadership Academy days, and I told her about how awful my summer was. She looked at me and said, "But you're Wonder Woman. We all look up to you. How can you not be strong? We need you."

I wanted to scream, "*That's not fair! Why do I have to be Wonder Woman?*" I would almost rather be damn Cinderella. Almost.

"Wonder Woman isn't real," I replied.

——

How many of you know a "Wonder Woman"? How many of you have been told you are "Wonder Woman"?

Wonder Woman's most noted superpower is her Lasso of Truth.

Let's try it out. Right now. You must answer truthfully because, you know, the Lasso of Truth.

LET'S START WITH A DEEP BREATH.

Are you OK?

SCAN YOUR BODY. BREATHE.

Are you really *OK?*

PAUSE. BREATHE.

What do you need to be OK?

PAUSE. BREATHE.

Sometimes you're not OK. And that's OK. Because Wonder Woman is not real.

HOW TO NOT BE WONDER WOMAN.

1. **Take up space.** Own your emotional state and space. It's OK to be mad. It's OK to be sad. Hell, it's even OK not to be OK. Say something. Let others in. And own your emotional intelligence. Don't let society use words that minimize our ability to feel, to connect, and to empathize. We do not create drama; we feel. We are not gossips; we connect. We are not weak; we

empathize. Like superstar New Zealand Prime Minister Jacinda Ardern says, "It takes strength to be an empathetic leader." How is your emotional intelligence a strength? Where can you use it to do the most good?

2. Be first. Talk about depression. Talk about how you're really doing; find the friend who is able to listen and be comfortable with the uncomfortable. And don't let others label you. "I'm not Wonder Woman. I'm Kristi, who right now is OK. But please do check back. Often." How are you really doing? Who can you reach out to?

3. Look for the helpers. Sometimes helpers are paid for. I have a therapist who helps me not to be a caretaker and to understand what Little Kristi needs to heal. The work I do in the world is disruptive; I'm not always liked. I have a group of women around the world who remind me that 1.) I don't have to be liked by everyone. 2.) They like me. What do you need to be OK?

NOW, DO SOMETHING THAT MAKES YOU FEEL MORE OK THAN YOU DID BEFORE READING THIS.

YOU'RE NOT READY; YOU'RE TOO READY.

Women's progress has been a collective effort.

—GLORIA STEINEM

ST. LOUIS, JULY 2013.

"When is your first class?" asked my fierce feminist friend Katie. I took out my calendar.

"September eighth. Eight weeks from today," I replied.

My friends Tracy, Katie, Amy, and I were gathered around a gorgeous, polished wooden dining room table passed down from Katie's meemaw. They were here to help me launch my yet-to-be-named business. They were graduates and friends of mine from Leadership Academy, class of 2004.

The Leadership Academy identified high-potential leaders in the community to grow us into future board members and community leaders. It was one of the inspirations for my business model because of the strong, powerful cohort. I could reach out to any of my cohort, and I would be encouraged, inspired, challenged, and sponsored, just like these women around the table.

"You don't have a curriculum. You don't have any students. You don't have a space. You don't have a name. You're not ready, Hemmer," my friends told me.

"I'm ready," I said, nodding my head vehemently. I thought to myself how even my powerful, changemaking friends around the table could benefit from my class, "Putting the W in Power." Starting my business felt more urgent than ever.

"Why don't you wait until spring semester?" Amy asked.

"I'll be in Bali by then; I want to launch in person. I'm doing it now," I said.

"Well, at least call Jim. And sign up for a business class," Katie suggested. Jim was our cohort's start-up expert.

I added "Call Jim" to my list, and we took a sugar break before tackling the next item on our list: business name. My original name, SUPERgirls Academy, did not work for two reasons: (1) my focus group told me that as women, they didn't want to be called girls, and (2) when my friends flew all over the country to help me with my business, they thought they would be helping me with a school for middle-school girls. There were plenty of programs for girls; there weren't many for women.

I ordered cupcakes from a woman-owned bakery with my brand-new business credit card, and we went back to Katie's fancy dining room. We discussed potential names, and up popped the word MOXIE.

"What is MOXIE?" I asked.

They looked at each other in disbelief. "How can somebody as well-read and smart as you not know this word?" Amy asked.

"Maybe it's a Southern thing?" I replied.

Katie disappeared and returned with the biggest dictionary ever, the kind libraries have on display. She paged through and read the definition: "MOXIE: force of character, nerve, energy. Synonyms: self-assurance, pluck, courage."

We looked at each other. This was me. Sorry, not sorry. Bossy, not bossy. Cruel, Heartless B*tch, not Cruel or Heartless or a B*tch.

"How about MOXIEboutique?" Tracy suggested.

"But I'm not selling clothing," I said.

We went back and forth for a bit, and then Tracy said, "I need some MOXIE." When we asked what was going on, she told us her dad wasn't doing well. "After losing his business, he lost his MOXIE. He's lost not only his identity but his support system."

Tears came. We listened. We embraced Tracy. "We're here for you," we said.

This. This. This was what my business was about. It didn't need a name. It didn't even need curriculum. It needed the space for women to show up unapologetically.

When I returned to Minneapolis, where I planned to pilot my business, I called Jim.

I told Jim I was starting a social enterprise that focused on women who were changemakers to provide them a safe space to unleash potential, take up space, and be powerful. I wanted to create the workplace of the future.

"Do you think I'm ready?" I asked.

He said, "If you're not embarrassed by your launch, you waited too long. Call me if you need anything else."

I had a double bind on my hands. My friends told me I wasn't ready; Jim told me that I was too ready. Lose-lose.

Roxane Gay in *Hunger* captured the double bind perfectly: "As a woman, as a fat woman, I am not supposed to take up space. And yet, as a feminist, I am encouraged to believe I can take up space. I live in a contradictory space where I should try to take up space but not too much of it."[1]

According to a 2018 article in the *Harvard Business Review*,[2] there are four double binds that keep women out of the C-suite.

- Double bind #1. Demanding yet caring. "Get results but don't be too intimidating."

1   Gay, Roxane. *Hunger: A Memoir of (My) Body.* New York: HarperCollins, 2017.
2   Zheng, Wei, Ronit Clark and Alyson Meister. "How Women Manage the Gendered Norms of Leadership." https://hbr.org/2018/11/how-women-manage-the-gendered-norms-of-leadership

- Double bind #2. Authoritative yet participatory. "Be the expert but not arrogant."

- Double bind #3. Advocating for themselves yet serving others. "Speak up for yourself but always put the team first."

- Double bind #4. Maintaining distance yet being approachable. "Be professional but be a friend at the same time."

As a principal, the barrier I struggled with most was #1: "Get results but don't be too intimidating." I was hired to be an "instructional leader" for 224 girls; I knew as a teacher and a counselor that what we did now impacted their confidence the rest of their lives. Although I had good results with the girls' academic and social well-being, some of the teachers were intimidated with my style and change of pace in how "things had always been done," and three resigned after my first year.

From that experience, now as a business owner, world traveler, and changemaker, I have learned to show my warmth before my strength. To me, that means getting results at my client's pace, not mine. Listening to what's important to my client before I show my expertise. Innovating to find a way to elevate the team, my impact, and the community at the same time. Connecting deeply and quickly with the stakeholders to build trust before I share what impact I can make for them.

Ironically, I have learned to slow down to go fast.

MINNEAPOLIS, AUGUST 2013.

In a conference room at an all-women university, my focus group shared their ideas for my business that still didn't have its first student or curriculum or name. Yet.

"AWE: Academy for Women's Empowerment," Kelli said.

42

"On a scale of one to ten, ten being highest, how much do you like the name?" I asked the group of seven changemaking women.

"Ten," said Shelly.

"Nine," said Grace

"Six or seven," said the coordinator of leadership at this university.

"Tell me more," I encouraged.

"It's too strong. It's too powerful. If you write you graduated from Academy for Women's Empowerment on your resume, you may not be hired." A double bind: be empowered but not powerful. The head of leadership at a women's university was afraid of power—that felt like another double bind.

Shelly chimed in, "But wouldn't that be a good thing? I wouldn't want to work at a place that was afraid of me and my level of empowerment."

Shelly held our attention; she was busting the double bind. "And Kristi, I'm going to be your first student. Sign me up!"

Shelly graduated from AWE's first class in 2013 and went on to start her own business about the pay gap. She freelances full time so she can work and raise her two children anywhere in the world, and she continues to stand in her power as a feminist, mom, and business owner.

What double bind are you going to bust?

#CHBs? MOXIEon. Not 100-percent ready? MOXIEon. Double binds? MOXIE THE HELL ON!

HOW TO BE READY WHEN YOU DON'T FEEL READY.

1. **Take up space.** Even if you're not ready, do it anyway. The classic research quoted in *Lean In* by Sheryl Sandberg shows that women wait and won't apply for a job until 100 percent ready. Men, 60

percent. One male manager I was working with laughed at that stat and said, "Try 15 percent." The world needs you to own your power and stop waiting like Cinderella. Be ready enough to start that business, go for the promotion, stand on that stage, speak up for yourself, leave a bad relationship. I was not embarrassed by my launch; I had six women, a beautiful space, and a MOXIElicious curriculum. What are you ready enough to do today?

2. Be first. If you're going to be first, you're going to need MOXIE. I need MOXIE to keep going when the big deal falls through. I need MOXIE when I'm told that the men and some of the women are resentful of the work I'm doing in their company. I need MOXIE when a pandemic shifts the way I do business. Be the first to MOXIEon. Show the world and more importantly show yourself that you can and will MOXIEon. How will you MOXIEon?

3. Look for the helpers. Amy and Katie continue to be part of AWE's development. Katie shared my programs at her company, and I was hired. Amy was inspired by my work and fought the government and won. They are allies; they are sponsors. But sponsors aren't just women. Jim was a sponsor. He not only told me to get going, but also hired me for his company to work with women in tech. He was my first business-to-business hire, which led to Mark hiring me for my first corporate gig. If you had told me when I quit teaching my next gig would be to change the power system of corporate America, I would have told you with all my self-assurance, "That's not possible." But that's what I do. Who are your sponsors?

RIGHT NOW, WHAT ARE YOU READY ENOUGH TO SAY YES TO?

DON'T (LET GIRLS) QUIT.

*Power can be taken, but not given. The process
of the taking is empowerment in itself.*

—GLORIA STEINEM

SOUTH DAKOTA, 2012.

"I'm going to quit telling everybody you're writing a book," my
mom said.

"Mom, I never told you to tell anybody I'm writing a book," I
replied.

"They keep asking me at work, and you're still not done."

Ever since I held my first "published" book, *The Funny Boy on
the Block*, in my hand as an eight-year-old at the Carnegie-Stout
Public Library in Dubuque, I knew I wanted to be an author.
Mrs. Berry's class project gave me not only a safe space to share
what was happening to me, but also a voice for others to be seen,
be heard, and change. Kristi the eight-year-old dreamed of having her books (plural) in libraries around the world, ready to be
checked out with a quick stop at the card catalog.

MINNEAPOLIS, 2020.

"I have something I want to talk to you about." It's an email from a woman I am an "auntie" to, Julie.

I met Julie when I presented *The Power of Presence* to the Women's Resource Group at her company. She was first in line telling me that the workshop had changed her life, and she wanted to learn more.

I was curious about her email and set up a coffee date to find out what she wanted to talk about and why she wanted to talk to me.

"How's the book going?" Julie asked before I could even sit down.

"It's hard," I replied.

"I'm so glad to hear you say that. I've been wanting to quit something myself."

She told me she was preparing for her MCAT: pre-med. Right now, she had a good job as an engineer at a good company, but she'd always wanted to work in medicine. She'd applied for pre-med right out of college and hadn't gotten in. Since then, she'd been preparing, not only studying for the MCAT but also volunteering at places that focused on women's and children's health.

"I see all my friends being successful. Making lots of money. Going out at night. I still live with my parents and stay home at night studying and spend my weekends volunteering." She sighed.

"What does the sigh tell you?" I asked.

"The sigh wonders, 'Are all the sacrifices worth it?'" Julie said. I got it; *Will the book be worth it?*

I shared with her the research about girls' confidence peaking at nine and girls dropping out of sports (and activities they love) at around fourteen. "We can't let girls quit."

I continued, "When I feel like quitting, I think of what Mary Wittenberg said: 'Don't let a girl quit. You can learn so much about yourself if you just don't quit. You learn that you have the will to continue on. Then, when someone or something down the line tries to stop you, you won't allow it.'

"I remind myself of this when I don't feel like writing after working all day. I'm learning so much about myself by not quitting," I said.

"Like what?" she asked.

"I have learned that I have something to say that matters, I am still a good writer, and it is worth it. Even if it doesn't get on the *NYT* bestsellers list," I added.

"Cool," Julie whispered.

"Writing this book is what eight-year-old Kristi would be doing right now if she were forty-nine going on fifty."

Relief spread through Julie's body. Her face relaxed, and she smiled.

"I find that girls are allowed to quit so much more than boys. Girls are comforted and boys are pushed. Just like the research shows that women are coached in confidence while their counterpart men are being coached in business, financial, and strategic acumen," I added.

In fact, according to a study from Cornell, women receive less negative feedback. "'Benevolent sexism' is not helpful," sums up the *British Psychological Society Research Digest*.[1]

"You're right! I was working on my taxes, and my dad said, 'Honey, let me help you with that'; my younger brother heard and asked for his help, and he said, 'Go into your room and figure it out.'"

"I can't quit! I already quit one dream in my life," Julie confided. When she was in her teens, she excelled at debate and international policy. She saw herself going to Columbia and studying public policy and changing the world. But then her parents were transferred to Minnesota, and she stayed there.

---

1   Stillman, Jessica. "New Study: Female Employees Receive Less Useful Feedback." https://www.inc.com/jessica-stillman/new-study-female-employees-receive-less-useful-feedback.html

"I'm doing it. I'm taking the test, and I will get into a school this time," Julie said.

"How can I support you?" I asked.

"I don't know yet."

"Can I check in on you?" She nodded. I added the date of her test into my calendar.

Another girl is not quitting.

EAST AFRICA, SUMMER 1995.

In 1994, my dad was diagnosed with leukemia. By then, Grandma Hemmer had died of lymphoma, which spread to her colon; Grandpa Hemmer had been diagnosed with prostate cancer, which later on would move to his bones; and Grandpa Linneman had died of kidney cancer that moved to his bones. I love math and numbers, but I did not love these numbers. Statistically, I was going to die young. Of cancer.

My realization that I could be genetically disposed to die young and National Geographic's IMAX "Africa: Serengeti inspired me to travel internationally for the first time. It was my second year of teaching, and I was enamored with the East African Nandi tale *Bringing the Rain to Kapiti Plain*, retold by Verna Aardema, about a farmer waiting for the annual rains. To make the story more accessible to my multicultural third-grade classroom in inner-city Houston, I brought in the African game of Mancala, invited my students from Africa to share traditional foods, and showed National Geographic's IMAX *Africa: The Serengeti*. The Serengeti called to me. I needed to experience the African rains, meet the Maasai farmers in the story, and get close and personal with the wildebeest. I would go on a safari to East Africa.

It took me over one year to save the money by working three jobs. I taught daily from 7:00 a.m. to 3:00 p.m., worked at a tutoring service from 3:30 to 6:00 p.m., and taught enrichment classes on Saturday from 1:00 to 4:00 p.m. to save the money for my safari. I booked through Micato Safaris because it was locally owned, and I'm proud to say it still exists and wins awards for being sustainable.[2] My twenty-three-year-old self hasn't changed much; I still choose companies that make social impact in their community.

On day four of my safari, we were headed out to the Serengeti when, in one life-changing moment, I spotted on one side a Maasai farmer tending the cattle just like *Bringing the Rains to Kapiti Plain*. On the other side, I saw Mt. Kilimanjaro rise from the earth. Our safari guide told us it was the largest mountain on the continent and could be climbed without rappelling. I told myself, "One day, I will return and climb Mt. Kilimanjaro."

MT. KILIMANJARO, SEPTEMBER 2003.

One day (eight years later), I returned to climb Mt. Kilimanjaro. When I arrived at the airport in Moshi, Tanzania, nobody was there to pick me up. I grabbed my overpacked, overstuffed backpack and plopped on a bench.

A friendly tour guide named Masa struck up a conversation and asked, "Are you going on the Coca-Cola or the Whiskey Trail?"

Confused, I replied, "I'm going on the Machame Trail."

"Ooh. That's the Whiskey Route. It's much harder than the Coca-Cola Route. You must be rugged."

I gulped. "Not really."

"Well, if you don't make it to the top, that's OK. You tried. It's getting late; you shouldn't be here by yourself. What company are you trekking with?"

2 Micato Safaris. https://www.micato.com/

I told him. He didn't recognize the name. "What's the phone number?" I dug in my backpack and found her number.

An hour later, my guide picked me up. I bid farewell to Masa and was taken to a small, dusty office in the town of Moshi. I found out that the four British men who I'd signed up with for a lower rate had canceled. I would still be charged the same rate but would be climbing alone. No other climbers, just my guide.

On the way up the steep creek beds, I cursed myself for not taking the Coca-Cola Route. My short legs struggled with the deep embankments, and the steep incline left me doubting myself. I was the last to arrive at the first camp. Two friendly British guys became my base-camp buddies, and as we were exchanging adventures from the day, they started puking from ascending too fast. While one puked, the other kept me company. Before we tucked in for the night, we got word that one of the guides had died on the mountain: aneurysm.

The next morning, the British chaps said, "We're going to climb with you, Kristi, so we don't puke. Your rate seems to work." After an hour of one foot—then the next—switchback—pause—repeat, they said, "We'll see you at camp," and abandoned me. That evening, we ate our popcorn and hot chocolate together, and they shared that my guide, Robert, was telling the other guides that he was "hooking up" with me. It didn't surprise me; I felt the invasive stares from the other guides. They said not to worry, that nobody believed it. We said our good-byes that evening because the next day they were heading up the Coca-Cola Route, and I was not. "Good luck, Kristi."

As I was trekking the next day, a Swiss woman caught up with me. She walked with me a bit and told me I was the only one trekking alone; the rest of her crew were wondering if I was OK doing this all alone.

Alone. I'm always alone. I went on the safari alone. I trekked Kili alone. I live alone. But I don't usually feel lonely.

We chatted for a bit, and then she trekked on. I felt really lonely. Although Robert was still technically with me, I did not feel comfortable with him, especially after the British guys told me what he was saying about me in camp. He trekked ahead of me.

At the next camp, Robert told me that a German man had died from complications with asthma; I wished I had prepared more. I dropped iodine pills into my floaty-laced river water, thankful my Nalgene bottle was bright yellow like my alma mater's color, not clear. If I could have seen what I was drinking, I'm not sure I could have done it.

Waiting for it to get late enough to go to bed, I met the Swedes: Denis, Andy, Carl, and Nickolas. They were avid climbers and invited me over to their tent to play cards, eat popcorn, and hang out. When I came back from the long drop, they dubbed me "Princess" because I was anything but a princess. I hadn't showered in four days, I used the long drop (and may or may not have always used toilet paper), I was sunburned from being so close to the sun, and I won all the games of cards. It was a term of endearment and pure irony. We said our good-lucks and went to bed extra early, as the next day was SUMMIT. They were opting to do a technical climb rather than the trail, so we wouldn't see each other again until camp. "Do the best you can, Princess. We love you no matter what."

My wake-up call was at 3:00 a.m.; I put on all my layers. It was windy, a cold I'd never experienced before, and I was from the tundra of the Midwest. It was never-ending shale. Take two steps, slide back one.

A glimpse of the summit gave me hope. I asked Robert, "How much longer?"

"Another three hours."

I was conflicted. I could see the top, but could I do another three hours? Was Robert telling me the truth? Or was he trying to get me to turn back early? At that moment, I felt so alone. Nobody would ever know. And nobody expected me to summit anyhow.

I turned around.

When I got back to camp, I hid in my tent from the shame of not summiting. I heard the victorious Swedes return and went outside to greet them. They shared their stories and their souvenir rocks from the summit.

"What's wrong, Princess?"

"I didn't make it to the top." Exhaustion and disappointment overwhelmed me. I was going to cry. They circled around me.

"You'll always be our Princess." And Denis reached in his pocket and gave me a piece of Kili (what you call the mountain if you've been in its presence).

I still have the rock. It no longer mocks me but reminds me to keep going. To believe in myself when nobody else does, or when expectations are set low for me because I'm a girl. Or when I'm being protected from hard stuff.

Do I want to go back and summit? Heck no.

I know I have it in me to do hard things. I score above 90 percent of all Americans on the Grit Quiz from Angela Duckworth's work.[3] I have MOXIE. The one word my niece uses to describe me is *determined*. So why did I quit climbing?

It wasn't too hard. I rafted the Zambezi River, sandboarded black-diamond sand dunes in Peru, swam with sharks in the Galapagos, and trekked the rainforests of Borneo with a broken foot bone. I can do very hard things.

For me, it was about belonging. Belonging is a human need that is hardwired into our DNA. I felt like an outsider; I wasn't included in the celebrations at base camp each night. Although I met people along the way, I still went back into my tent at night alone, climbed Kili alone, and didn't summit alone.

It's also about low expectations that are put on girls and women. "Here's the thing about girls, and all children, actually:

---

3   Duckworth, Angela. "Grit Scale." https://angeladuckworth.com/grit-scale/

They see no limits to their potential until adults point them out," says Lori Day in her *HuffPost* blog post "The Soft Bigotry of Low Expectations for Girls."[4] I would add women too.

I believed I could climb Kili. I wanted to climb Kili. But as soon as I landed, I was told by everyone from the helpful guide Masa in the airport to my Swedish friends on the way up that it was OK if I didn't make it.

To me, the low expectations were also a form of protection: protection from failure. Masa, the Brits, and the Swedes didn't want me to feel failure, the big F-word for women.

Back then, quitting felt shameful. When I told people I'd climbed Kili, I never mentioned the itty-bitty detail that I hadn't actually summited. I had the rock in my pocket.

Now, the quitting feeling reminds me not to let others "protect" me from failure. Like my friends who thought I wasn't ready to start my business, or friends asking if I was going to quit on my business and go back to teaching when COVID hit. The quitting feeling tells me to push on when it matters. Run one more minute. Write one more proposal. Listen one more time. Revise until I'm proud. Summit.

Today, I am somebody who won't let other girls and women quit. I'm a source of belonging for other girls and women like Julie. And I stretch expectations—not lower them. I will not be the limit to their potential.

Right now, the world needs us to create a future where the potential of girls and women is not limited.

Don't quit.

HOW TO NOT QUIT.

1. **Take up space.** Don't quit on your dream. And don't let oth-

---

4   Day, Lori. "The Soft Bigotry of Low Expectations for Girls." *Huffington Post*. https://www.huffpost.com/entry/the-soft-bigotry-of-low-expectations-for-girls_b_3573702

ers' expectations limit you. Do your MOXIEst work. Do your most "powerful beyond measure" work. Your greatest good for the greatest good. Summit. What dream must you never quit?

Note of caution: Sometimes taking up space means to have the guts to QUIT. The bad job. The bad boss. The bad relationship. Know the difference. Quitting my job when I was principal was how I got my agency back. Quitting climbing Kilimanjaro was not.

2. Be first. To go on a safari. To climb Mt. Kilimanjaro. To get your master's. To sacrifice for what you really want. Whenever I feel like I'm not successful enough, I don't have enough followers, it's too much sacrifice, it's too much rejection, or nobody cares, I think about Twitter. One of its founders once shared that everyone believes that Twitter was an "overnight success," but what everyone doesn't know is that it took thirteen years to get there. Don't quit. What first is worth all the sacrifice?

3. Look for the helpers. The guide at the airport saved me from a disaster. My trekking company forgot about me. This was 2003, before smartphones and before the internet became all pervasive. The two British guys welcomed me and even tried trekking with me. The Four Swedes made me part of their team; I know if one of them had been with me, I would have summitted. I needed a sense of belonging.

For me, belonging also comes from the audiences I stand in front of. The strangers that tell me to hurry up and finish the book so that they can read it and buy a copy for their daughters and husbands too. Belonging comes from my friends who have read so many versions of this, and my editor Amy, who even though she wanted it to be called *Three Simple Ways to Dismantle Patriarchy* still believed and stuck with me.

Belonging also comes in email form. One of my clients wrote, "Kristi, take your time. We will wait for you."

Even if I'm the last one to summit. What is worth waiting for?

DON'T QUIT. AND DON'T LET OTHER GIRLS QUIT.

P.S. This book is dedicated to my mom, Linda Kay Linneman Hemmer, who didn't quit believing in me and who can now share *Quit Being So Good* all over Facebook.

WHAT IT'S LIKE FOR A GIRL IN THIS WORLD.

Empathy is the most radical of human emotions.

—GLORIA STEINEM

"Not getting raped was the most avid hobby of my youth," says Rebecca Solnit in her book *Recollections of My Nonexistence*.[1] I would add, not getting raped **or killed.**

HOUSTON, 1990s.

My teaching colleague showed me bruises from falling in the bathtub when she was drunk. Why did one bruise look like a handprint? "I'm so lucky Bo was there to help me," she said. My hands got sweaty. My heart beat faster. I was holding my breath. I knew from my training at the Houston Area Women's Center that my colleague was being physically abused, probably emotionally and financially too.

My friend from graduate school called me and whispered, "I'm afraid, next time, he's going to kill me." She was not ready to leave him then (on average, it takes seven times to leave an

---

[1]   Solnit, Rebecca. *Recollections of My Nonexistence*. New York: Viking, 2020.

abusive partner before it's for good), so how could we keep her and her children safe?

"Jen, let's pack your emergency bag together right now," I said. We packed the bag, and she hid it for the next time.

<hr>

Every hour around the world, six women are killed by a family member or partner.

If you open up the headlines from any day in any country with a free press, you will find a consistent percentage about violence against women. On the day I was writing this, the headline was from NBC News: "Florida child's mother shot and killed during online Zoom class as teacher watches." The shooter was a man the mother used to date.

Today when I was revising this story, the headline that caught my eye (there were many to choose from in my Facebook feed) was a repost from Amanda Goodman of Family & Children's Council.

> Sydney Sutherland went for a jog in Arkansas.
> She was murdered.
> The past few days I've read things like, "She shouldn't have run alone," "Hopefully she had more than a sports bra on," "Why did she take that route?" and "Women should carry Mace with them."
> How about we say this: stop killing women.
> We should be able to walk, jog, shop or do anything in between without looking over our shoulders.
> We're not inferior objects free for the taking.
> We're not yours to take.
> God bless her family and friends.

I googled the story, and this headline popped up first. "Arkansas woman killed while running: what women should know to stay safe on outdoor runs."[2] Blaming the victim.

This is what it's like for a girl in this world. Murdered while running in broad daylight in a neighborhood you grew up in, and you're blamed and told to do better next time. But you can't do better because this time, you're dead. There is no next time.

———

KOH SAMUI, THAILAND, 2006.

Do you know what it feels like in this world, for a girl?

Madonna does. She sang about the paradox of being a girl: "Strong inside, but you don't know it. Good little girls, they never show it. When you open up your mouth to speak, could you be a little weak?" She asked, "Do you know what it feels like in this world. For a girl?"

I ask, "At the Green Mango in Koh Samui, Thailand?"

After quitting my really bad job as a principal in a Southern town, I told everybody I was going to take a year off and write a book. It was true—I wrote a book, *BE: A Year of Being*, but I didn't publish it.

That year gave me the freedom to travel around the world, live on twenty dollars a day, and tick "writer" on the customs form. My friends decided to visit me in one of my favorite places in the world: Koh Samui. We kayaked the Gulf of Thailand, visited an elephant sanctuary, and ate up all the colorful fruits like jackfruit, rambutan, and mangosteen. I challenged them to durian, and my friend's daughter Emmy accepted.

On Emmy's last night in Koh Samui, I took her down Mango Street to experience Thai nightlife, because her mom asked me

2   Bernable, Angeline Jane, and Suzanne Yeo. "Arkansas woman killed while running: What women should know to stay safe on outdoor runs." ABC News. https://abcnews.go.com/GMA/News/arkansas-woman-killed-running-women-stay-safe-outdoor/story?id=72560802

(well, actually told me) to take Emmy out for a night on Mango Street before they returned. She trusted I would keep Emmy safe and yet show her a fun time. I agreed with her—I was trustworthy, and we would have fun. Keeping her safe in this world was what I was worried about. If you're a woman, you know how the story goes. You have lived it. If you're a man, keep reading.

Walking down the strip littered with cabarets, nightclubs, sex workers, drugs, and party-mongers, we immediately drew attention. A random guy yelled, "What are you two doing by yourselves?" Emmy looked at him. I didn't. Technically, we were not by ourselves (see Rule Number Three below). We were with each other. Translated English to English, "What are you doing without a man?" was what he was really asking.

As her elder (I was thirty-five, she was twenty-one), I felt I must impart my well-earned wisdom and also wanted to make sure she made it back to her room and to her mom without being raped or killed. I said to Emmy, "There are three rules I want you to remember."

As I was an "auntie," she listened intently to me and my wisdom. "Number One. Thailand is a lot different than any other place you've been in America. That's a good thing and a bad thing. Remember, we own our experience. We own our YES, and more importantly, we own our NO. Period.

"Number Two. Do not accept any open drinks from boys. If they buy us a drink, it must come from a bottle, and one of us will watch to make sure the date rape drug isn't slipped in it." She nodded. I wondered what she was thinking.

"Number Three. We must always stay together. If you go to the bathroom, I go with you. If you want to dance with a cute boy, and his friend is ugly, I have to dance with the ugly boy.

"That's it. If we follow these three rules, we should be just fine."

But I forgot about being a girl in this world—the subtleties that are just part of that. I didn't warn her about these:

- You will be objectified. Push back.

- Guys will assume you should smile at their stupid, belittling jokes. Don't smile. Or deflect it by saying, "You smile."

- You will be expected to dance with whoever asks you to. You don't have to. Only dance with those you want to dance with.

- Men's main feeling after entitlement is anger. Stay out of the anger. Bad happens there. Don't appease, but exit. Get out!

Women talk about work-life balance. That's not what kills us. It's a balancing act of speaking up and doing what you really want along with not getting harassed, beat up, or killed. If you think I'm exaggerating, right now, go to your favorite news source; check the headlines. Of the ten-plus headlines, at LEAST one of them will be about a woman or girl being killed, raped, harassed, or bullied by a man.

I was fighting a hard battle. Society had already trained Emmy to be tolerant, appeasing, apathetic, and accommodating. From my experience as a teacher, counselor, and principal, I knew girls and the women they grew up into.

We got a great table at Sweet and Soul Café right by the street and ordered two national beers, Singhas. People-watching is the best on Mango Street. The first character that caught our attention was an older, very pale, Buddha-bellied, bald-headed man who had on a shredded cotton T-shirt. He walked like Frankenstein's monster and turned out to be just as dangerous. He had a problem with pinching Thai girls' butts. When the Goon lumbered toward them, they immediately backed up against the wall, denying him access. They knew him. A regular entitled man of the oldest, grossest kind.

Goon tried to enter our bar, but the security guard denied him access to hundreds of butts. He shoved his hands in his pockets and tried to enter again. However, the security guard knew that putting his hands in his pockets was just a trick. He didn't plan to keep them there long.

Emmy and I watched as he wandered the street. When we stopped homing in on his whereabouts, he took the opportunity and lumbered toward our table. Our bums were firmly planted and protected on our wooden chairs, but he leaned in and wiggled his fingers over our table and mumbled something. I instinctively yelled, "Get away." He moved away, but I was resentful of the fear pulsing through my veins. I was responsible not only for my safety but Emmy's too. Why couldn't he just leave us alone? All of us girls. Jerk!

We headed to the dance floor for refuge and were about to stick our big toes out when a dark and handsome guy wearing a white T-shirt and a man-bag quickly approached me. He leaned in and asked in an Israeli accent, "Are you in the army?" My camo skirt must have triggered the pickup line, along with his most likely being on holiday after his mandatory army service. He was programmed for fatigues.

"I'm undercover," I snapped back coyly. He smiled, but then I deflected him. I was with Emmy and needed to stick to our three rules. If I gave this guy any attention, he'd hang onto us the rest of the night, and we had just got there. I turned away and chatted with Emmy, intentionally ignoring him. He walked away.

We stepped out onto the dance floor, and three guys swarmed around us. We no longer had any space to dance. All I wanted to do was dance and have fun with Emmy on her last night. The three guys tried to gyrate against us. We slithered away into the crowd.

Emmy was dangerous. She was young and fresh and giggled. She innocently looked around and met stares constantly, which of course brought a larger crowd swarming around us. And as luck would have it, my Israeli friend came back with a buddy. He was friendly, eager, and probably in his early twenties.

His name was Leo, and he had just arrived. He was eager to have fun, but I was with Emmy and it was her last night. Again, they left the scene. Emmy leaned in and told me she'd followed Rule Number Two—Leo's friend had offered a sip from his drink and she'd said no. I was so thankful I'd told her not to drink anything unprotected and that she was good at following directions.

There was a really bad dancer who kept moving in to join us. He had a white ringer shirt with "Woolrich" on it. He had on tight jeans and really bad shoes. He did a little shuffle, one foot to the other, and was just hopeless. I started watching him, and Emmy and I both felt sorry for him. Almost sorry enough to invite him to dance with us. He seemed harmless. But we decided not to, as we'd be stuck with him the rest of the night.

One nearby dancer in a royal-blue tank top, cut-off jean shorts, high white socks with matching royal-blue stripes, and tan buck suede construction boots that had been fashionable in the '90s punched his fists in the air in some male dominance dance and brushed up against us several times. He was trouble; we moved away.

Then a random man quickly jumped between the two of us and tried to gyrate with me. He was upset at my inattention, which he read as rejection (rightly so), and said something to Emmy about how hostile I was or something like that. He told me to "smile" and moved on. When he left, I smiled. How would he like to be harassed constantly by drunk, unattractive men who think that all women should be with them?

As I was wondering this, a guy walked by and brushed my bum, then my shoulder, then my face all in one swoop. How he managed this, I don't know. He turned around to see if I was interested, and I looked at him like, "*Who the hell do you think you are?*" He continued to the bathroom and didn't return.

11:00 p.m. We decided it was time to head to the Green Mango; it had filled up in the past hour. We headed to the bar and sat down at a picnic table. Before we had a chance to order a drink, a Swedish guy swooped down on Emmy and chatted her up, offering to buy her a drink. She ordered us each a beer; when they were brought over, she leaned over and let me know proudly that she saw them uncapped, so they were safe. Her innocence e reminded me of my little sisters, and I missed them.

I saw the Swede's friend standing against the bar, checking me out. He came over and sat next to me on the bench. I guess I passed. He was cute. I'd noticed him earlier at the other place. However, he wasn't the sharpest tool in the shed, or he was just that drunk. He slurred so that it was almost impossible to understand what he was saying.

But I don't think words were on his mind. Initially, we talked about Koh Samui, his friends, traveling, his job working with horse feed. He had lovely blue eyes, bronzed skin, nice white teeth, and sun-kissed blond hair. He was a cutie. But, alas, he put his hand on my back and then my bum. Thankfully, he was a little brighter than I'd originally believed, as he got the hint when I winced and moved away from his touch—he left.

2:00 a.m. We'd been subjected to the world for over four hours. I was exhausted and worn out from keeping Emmy safe. It was time to go home.

As we were walking back among the sex workers, madness, and party vibe, men called at us, "Where are you going, honey?"

When we turned into her hotel, a random guy yelled, "Good night!"

We didn't respond. Emmy was learning.

I dropped her off and headed the couple of blocks to my hostel. Two guys were leaving a bar and got on their motorbikes. One yelled, "Good night!" I was pretty sure he was talking to me, although I'd never met him or set eyes on him before. I ignored him.

"Good night!" he yelled again. I still ignored him. "Good night!" he yelled a third time. To shut him up and avoid the anger I referred to above, I returned the good-night, and he got on his bike and took off. I walked a little faster to my hostel. Although I was not afraid of being attacked openly, as there were more people on the streets of Koh Samui at 2:00 a.m. than there were at 10:00 a.m., I wanted to get out of this jungle.

I was about to turn down the road to my hostel when a man yelled, "Sweet dreams." I turned around and acknowledged him so he'd leave me alone. I didn't want to aggravate him and have him see what room I went into. That appeased him, and he was on his way.

Now, some of you may be thinking that all this attention must feel nice. Women can tell you that NO, it doesn't. It's power. Control. And it brings more often a rush of fear than pleasure.

Some of you may be thinking it was because I was in Thailand, where there's a lot of public and accepted prostitution. These experiences aren't unique to Thailand. In fact, in the sixty-five countries I've been to solo, I've been objectified, harassed, and feared for my physical safety in every single place.

And some may be wondering what I was wearing. I can wear anything I damn well please and deserve to be left alone in peace. When guys are wearing nasty Speedos, which is probably the least amount of clothes possible without being naked, they're not continuously harassed.

Then, there are some of you who may be wondering why I take things so seriously. Why not laugh it off? Would you want to spend the rest of the night stuck with any of the men I described? And more importantly, these seemingly benign or covert male behaviors lead to more overt behaviors like kidnapping a woman who is running in broad daylight, sexually assaulting her, murdering her, and burying her on your farm.

So, that's what it's like to be a girl in this world. Emmy and I just wanted to go out and have a good time without being harassed, assaulted, raped, or killed. But women, you already knew this.

about the men? Did you know that every hour around ᵗʰᵉ six women are killed by a partner or family member?

ᵗⁱᵃ Steinem says, "If you add up all the forms of genocide, from female infanticide and genital mutilation to so-called honor crimes, sex trafficking, and domestic abuse, everything, we lose about six million humans every year just because they were born female."

Six million females every year. We must do better. Let's make the world safer for women and girls.

HOW TO MAKE THE WORLD A SAFER PLACE FOR WOMEN AND GIRLS.

1. Take up space. Women, take up space at the polls. Vote people in who are making the world safer for women and girls. Vote for those who are upholding Title IX and the Violence Against Women Act and fighting for the Equal Rights Amendment (ERA). And hell's bells, run for office yourself. You're not alone; organizations like She Should Run[3] are there to help.

Men, use your space to make more space for women. Intentionally look around the boardroom—are there a variety of voices, or is it an echo chamber? Intentionally invite women, BIPOC, LGBTQ people, and other voices to the boardroom and then create a safe space for them to speak and be heard. Change "how things have always been done."

2. Be first. Women, with all the pressure to say YES, be first to say NO. No to the guy you don't really like. No to leading the committee that's not going to help your career. No to picking up the cake that's really not on your way home for the work party. Don't smile if you don't feel like it. And be the first to brag on another woman coworker in public. Be a role model for what is possible.

Men, now that you know better, do better, damn it! Your

---

3   https://www.sheshouldrun.org/

three rules: (1) You're not entitled to a yes. If you feel angry with a no, that's entitlement. Check yourself. (2) Say something if a friend is harassing a woman, talking about drugging women, or abusive in relationships. Help keep us safe and alive. (3) Listen. No means no.

3. Look for the helpers. Women, support, sponsor, and believe each other. And don't just stay with your friend when she's going to the bathroom, but buy her a ticket to that innovative event you were invited to. Call your colleague up and invite her to sit next to you at the changemaking meeting you're part of. Bring her along in your success. Sponsor her.

Men, know more. Get rid of your limiting beliefs and echo chambers. Ask your women friends, colleagues, and loved ones what makes them feel unsafe and then ask for tips on how to make them feel safe. One of my favorite tips my friend Jillian taught her husband and son is, "When it's dark out, never walk behind a woman; cross the street so it's very clear she's safe." Read books by Gloria Steinem, Angela Davis, and Sandra Cisneros. Follow UN Women, A Mighty Girl, and Malala on social media.

NOW THAT YOU KNOW BETTER, DO BETTER.

P.S. Here are two resources for you or others (women and men): healthline.com/health/sexual-assault-resource-guide and Rainn.org.

WHAT'S IN YOUR EMERGENCY BAG?

The caste systems of sex and race are interdependent and can only be uprooted together.

—GLORIA STEINEM

JAKARTA, 12 OCTOBER 2002.

Before Bollywood was popular, there was Mali. She was on the same Student Service Team as me at the international middle school where we both worked. Like me, she loved to write, dance, and sing karaoke. For her birthday, she rented a party room in downtown Jakarta for about ten of us.

The women around the table were from Mali's life from around the world. From her early childhood days, Meg from England. From her secondary school days, June from Singapore. Family friends from India. And me—the only American.

As the biggest Michael Jackson fan, Mali finished her rendition of "Beat It." Spirits were high. Voices were higher. We were having a fun night. One that we needed after all the restrictions and unknowns of living in Indonesia after 9/11—the first anniversary had barely passed.

"Hemmer! You're up. What song?" Mali asked.

"'Material Girl!'" I said.

Mali was scrolling through the song list to find the Madonna classic when June's phone rang. She was a big-time journalist for Bloomberg; she took the call. We turned down the music a bit because it was never a good thing if she got a call at 1:00 a.m. from work—ever.

I watched as she nodded her head, looked at us, looked down, and stepped outside. We looked at each other and pretended it was OK, but we knew it wasn't.

A minute or so later, June walked back in and motioned for us to turn down the volume. "There's been a bombing in Bali. Outside the American embassy," she said.

Silence. BREATHE. IN. OUT.

"I have to leave. Sorry, Mali, for ruining your party."

Hugs all around. When she leaned in to hug me, she said, "Kristi, you need to come with me. I don't know what's going on, but you're American. We need to get you home safely."

BREATHE. IN. OUT.

"I'll have my driver drop me off at the office and then take you home."

BREATHE. IN. OUT.

"Thanks, June," Mali and I said in unison.

I sprinted with June as we left the club and got in her car. She gave directions in Bahasa Indonesia to her driver; he looked at me, worried too. He dropped her off at the office and drove me another forty-five minutes to my house.

I saw him looking at me in his rearview mirror. I recognized the look; he was worried about my safety. Like the majority of Indonesians, he cared about all who lived in Indonesia.

I started to worry. *Is my emergency bag packed?* After 9/11, we'd been instructed to have an emergency bag packed in case we needed to evacuate last minute. *Do I have enough rupiah at the house in case I need to evacuate? Or did I spend it again? Did I put my passport back in the emergency bag after I returned from Singapore?* I couldn't remember.

I was holding my breath. We pulled up to my house. BREATHE. IN. OUT.

I tried to give June's driver a tip for driving me forty-five min-

70

utes out and then forty-five minutes back in. He refused. *"Terima kasih, pak* [thank you, sir]," I said. He waved at me. It was 2:30 a.m.

―――

MINNEAPOLIS, 2020.

I knew what to pack when I lived in Jakarta in case we would be helicoptered out in the middle of the night. I knew what to pack in case of an earthquake when I lived in Tokyo. As a counselor, I knew how to coach women on what to pack in their emergency bag to get out safe if their partner was violent. On the brink of a coup in Kathmandu, I knew how to navigate the chaos with the help of my Nepalese friends. I know emergency bags.

However, living only a few miles away from the site of George Floyd's murder, I started wondering. *What's in the emergency bag of my Black friends? Specifically, my Black female friends.* They weren't going to be helicoptered out of racism, white supremacy, and sexism.

I think about having brunch with my friend Tracy at a popular spot in Chicago. She told me, "Normally, as a Black woman, I'd be mad we were put in back by the kitchen. But it's the only table open, so I'll let it pass."

As a white woman, I pay close attention to what gender gets seated or served before me, but I have never thought about the significance of where I was seated. This is privilege.

If Black history was readily taught, people like me would be more aware of the significance of being seated in the back for my Black friend. Just like women's history, Black history is often highlighted one month a year (if at all), when it is in fact integral to all aspects of American history.

I think about Grace, who says that she's tired of the assumptions of what it feels like to be a Black woman. She says it's rare for a white friend or white family member to ask her how she's feeling or what it's like because it's hard for white people to listen. To hear the pain and suffering.

And I think of my friend Cassandra, who I met in a small group discussion about economic equity for women in 2017. We came up with a plan for what to share with the group, and Cassandra volunteered to present our ideas to the larger group. When it was our turn, she said, "White women are the problem for Black women."

Huh? I thought. My mind raced: *I showed up today. I vote for candidates who support women. I stand up to sexism. I am a Seeking Educational Equity and Diversity trainer. I have a large network filled with women from all over the world and all walks of life. I stand up to racism. Right?*

I could feel my face get hot as I defended myself in my head. And then I paused and wrote down her name and email. Something was stirring inside of me. Something that I knew I couldn't let pass. Why was I angry? Because she hadn't followed the group rules? Because she didn't report back what we discussed in the group? Or was it because what I believed about me wasn't true? Was it possible that white women are the problem for Black women? After the meeting, there was a line to talk to her. I left with her email on the handout that sat in my file drawer with all my other good intentions.

A month later, a member of the chamber of commerce's economic equity committee I was on said, "I have a friend you need to meet." It was Cassandra.

He introduced us, and we met up. And met up again. And again. When I was asked by an influential international women's NGO to gather a group of women entrepreneurs, I invited Cassandra. I saved a spot for her next to me because I knew we would need to lead together.

Cassandra was not the only woman of color I invited who showed up; another was from Asia, another from South America. Of the fifteen women in the room, ten of them were from my network. As the entrepreneurs described some of the barriers of patriarchy, Cassandra said, "And let's not forget race."

A woman I hadn't invited said, "I have never seen racism in Minneapolis." She was born in Germany and had lived in the USA for over twenty years; she was white.

Cassandra added, "White women are the problem too."

The German woman raised her voice a bit more, stated her past experience as a high executive in finance from a fancy-schmancy company we all recognized, and said, "Not me; it's not true."

Cassandra replied, "Yes, you. All white women."

The woman went on and on. Cassandra said under her breath, "I can't stay. I am not going to listen to her."

I interrupted, "We need to pause. If a person says that this is her experience, another person cannot say otherwise. We must listen and ask questions."

One of the other women I invited chimed in, "This is what feminists do. We believe each other."

I added, "Who else has had experiences like Cassandra's around race they'd like to share?"

My friend from Nepal agreed with Cassandra, and the meeting ended with us agreeing that there was an intersection of gender and race that needed to be explored more.

Once the meeting was over, everybody stayed and connected. And connected. And connected.

I saw the German woman line up to talk to Cassandra; the teacher instinct in me moved close enough to hear in case Cassandra would need me again. She said, "I hope I didn't offend you."

"You did," Cassandra replied.

"What can I do?" the woman asked.

Without skipping a beat, Cassandra said, "You need to listen."

The German woman nodded, and I moved away. I was not needed.

LISTENING.

That's what I needed to do more of with Tracy. In fact, recently Tracy told me that what Black women mostly seek is the opportunity to be heard. That's what Grace craves—to be listened to. And it's the lesson Cassandra gave not only the German woman and me but all of us working on creating a more equitable and safer world.

Listening is foundational to leading with empathy. As a teacher, I taught and modeled for my students, and now with my clients, that there are three levels of listening: with their heads, ears, and hearts.

Listening with your head is the first level and is focused more on what you are going to say next, not on the other. This is not helpful for empathy.

Listening with your ears is the second level. You're focused on the other; you mirror their words and reflect what they are saying. You pay more attention to the other than yourself.

Where empathy can really happen is the third level: listening with your heart. You drop into the other person and feel what they are saying. You mirror their breathing. You ask powerful questions to understand, are present in the moment with the other, and trust your heart to listen until there is understanding.

With the USA struggling with social justice and COVID turning our world into a virtual reality, listening with your heart is more important than ever.

What is in your emergency bag?

What do we need in the world's emergency bag to make the world safer and more equitable for all? Specifically, what do Black women need?

I am listening with my heart.

HOW TO BE AN ADVOCATE.

1. Take up space. To make mistakes. My friends who are Black women will call me out if, as a white woman, I mess up because they have experienced racism; I have not. When they help me, I can use my white privilege to help another white person hear a different perspective, from reaching out personally to friends who say racist things on social media to speaking the truth about police brutality at a dinner party. What mistake are you willing to make to create a safer space for all?

2. Be first. To listen. A high school friend, Tony, once questioned the need for the Women's March on Facebook. I heard his question, and I private-messaged him. "Tony, I saw your post, and I'd love to share with you the importance of the Women's March."

He responded right away, "It's because I saw that you were there in DC that made me wonder if I was missing something because you stand up for things that are important. Even in high school. My daughter is a feminist like you."

I responded, "Let's talk! I can help you understand and support her as a dad."

"I will be sure to contact you if she or I need anything," he wrote back.

My goal wasn't to change how he voted or even make him become a feminist. My goal was for him to be an ally, to be a more empathetic dad, and to continue to be curious. Who do you need to listen to for better understanding?

3. Look for the helpers. June took the lead in Jakarta. She thought not only of her job, the incident, and consequences, but me as the only American in our party room. Her driver made me feel safe and cared about. Even though I was the only American and white woman in the group, I was not alone. People are watching out for me, and I'm watching out for you. What helpers and organizations are helping white people be anti-racist? And how do we spread their good work?

WHEN THINGS FEEL SCARY, BE THE FRIEND WHO SAVES HER A SEAT NEXT TO YOU.

P.S. In addition to saving a seat and saying something, here are resources for those of you who are working toward an inclusive world: Southern Poverty Law Center (splcenter.org); Teaching Tolerance (tolerance.org); and, for those of you who are white, here is an extra resource on how to be anti-racist— "First Listen. Then Learn: Anti-Racism Resources for White People," published by Forbes.com.

GET ON THE ROOF; OTHERS WILL FOLLOW.

*The future depends entirely on what each of us does
every day; a movement is only people moving.*

—GLORIA STEINEM

"It's hard to be what you can't see," Madeline Wright Edelman once said. She was right. It's much easier when you can see: Sally Ride flying in space. Maya Lin designing national monuments. Hillary Clinton vying for president. Sara Blakely creating a billion-dollar business from five thousand dollars—and then giving so much money away that she's no longer a billionaire. When you see it, it's easier to think, *If she can do it, I can too.*

When I was in elementary school, recess taught me an important lesson about space and my place: the Boys' Field and the Girls' Field. The Boys' Field was straight out the door, down the hill to a flat play area that went on and on and on. From afar, I would watch the boys play football, crack-the-whip, and run-across. The Girls' Field was on the side of the school, up a hill with a small play area, and out of the way. I didn't like it. It was in the shade, so it was always a bit chilly. It took up more precious recess time to get there, and when you got there, there was nothing to do. It was inconvenient. It was uninviting.

It clearly was not as important. As a problem solver, I deduced that this delineation meant girls clearly were not as important to the school as boys.

Although we weren't forbidden from the Boys' Field (this was barely after Title IX), the girls stayed in their place: on the blacktop or the Girls' Field. We were away from the action, the adventure, where important decisions were being made.

On the outskirts of the Boys' Field was the legendary Eagle's Nest—a mix of metal triangles that crested way into the sky, at least six feet. We girls were warned about its dangers; it was where the ice packs from the school nurse came from. It was where casts came from. It was where the boys played. I longed to climb the Eagle's Nest. To see the view from the top.

When I was in second grade, I got tired of playing on the boring blacktop isolated from all the fun, and I ran with the boys to the Eagle's Nest. I clenched the cold metal bar, lifted myself up, and started climbing. And climbing. And climbing. Until I was at the top. I didn't need help. I didn't end up in the nurse's office. I didn't feel scared; I felt powerful.

The next day, I ran straight to the Boys' Field, to the Eagle's Nest, and started climbing. Other girls saw me, and they milled around the Eagle's Nest. Climbing was fun, but tag was more fun. I played tag with the boys on the Eagle's Nest and called out to the girls to join us.

Today, I know as an early childhood professional that children intuitively climb as high as they feel comfortable with. They typically don't fall off the jungle gym until their mom or dad or teacher gasps and yells, "Be careful. You're going to fall." It's when doubt is introduced that the child will fall and break her arm, and then the adults will believe they are right.

Just like the corporate jungle gym: the women watch from below as the men climb to the top while they are instilled with fears and doubts. "Don't look too ambitious, nobody will like you." "How will you climb the jungle gym and have a family?"

And most destructive of all, "Don't fall!" When doubt is introduced to the woman, the woman falls—mentally. Game over.

In elementary school, the messages became our foundation. Stay in your place: the Girls' Field is where you won't be seen or heard, out of the way. You're not meant to be brave: stay on the ground, watch the boys do the dangerous stuff from afar, and you won't fail or get hurt. And *definitely* do not do better than the boys.

Stay in your place. But what happens when you don't? When you climb the Eagle's Nest? Excel in science? Travel the world alone? Don't follow the rules? A lot happens. You become memorable. And more importantly, you take up your space in the world. Which gives permission for other women and girls who are watching to do the same.

NEW ZEALAND, 1999.

I didn't want to party like it was 1999. And I wasn't going to shrink in fear of Y2K. I wanted to make an impact and be the first to see the new millennium. The first to see the sun rise. I like to be first.

New Zealand was first. They would welcome the new millennium with the first sunrise and be the first to experience Y2K—the ending of the world. I did some research on Yahoo (pre-Google days) for international travel over the turn of the century. Habitat for Humanity was doing a fourteen-day build over the New Year in Gisborne, New Zealand, alongside the indigenous Maori. We would welcome the new year and the new millennium with the traditional Maori boat ceremony. We would do a building blitz of three houses in one week, and afterward we'd whitewater raft, blackwater raft, and cliff dive. I signed up.

Our team of ten met at LAX before making the fifteen-hour

flight to Auckland. We were three women and six men plus our fearless female leader. A motley crew of college students, teachers, entrepreneurs, and corporate burnouts, we discovered we all had the same building experience: none. We landed on Christmas Day and made our way to the build site in Gisborne.

I had been on a group tour of East Africa, visited the Galapagos, and backpacked Europe by this point. I hadn't racked up the sixty-five countries I have today, but I had done enough group travel to understand the importance of being a team player. Even though I prefer solo travel, I followed the safety rules and made sure that my behaviors and choices didn't negatively impact my team.

The house we were mainly going to be working on had three bedrooms occupied by five children and their parents. The color swatches were bright and happy: sky blue, purple passion, cotton candy, and lily pad.

Day One: I wore my tool belt and had my leather gloves on, ready for action. The foreman looked at our collective group of about fifty from around New Zealand and the world and assigned us roles. The men to the left; the women to the right. The Boys' Field; the Girls' Field. The men grabbed their tools and headed to the wooden platforms to start framing, and the women picked up paintbrushes and headed to the corner in the chilly shade. I noticed the divide immediately, but my team player kicked in, and I stayed in my place.

We primed the wooden planks that would be used for the siding from 8:00 a.m. until our tea break at 10:00 a.m. While I enjoyed the conversation and mesmerizing strokes, I welcomed the break and checked on how far the house had come along. I waited for instructions to switch up roles. None. My insides started to roar, but I coached myself, *Be a team player. Be culturally appropriate. Stay in your place.* I flip-flopped from listening to stories to telling myself stories about all the times I'd been told by society to cook, not plane; pick up a paintbrush, not a hammer; be the assistant—not in charge.

Lunch arrived. The men came back tired and sweaty from building; the women were dirty and tired of being told to disappear into the corner with a paintbrush, supervised by an old, white man to keep us from laughing too loudly and dissenting. Well, that's how this woman felt, anyway.

After lunch, any hope I had of building was sent to the corner to paint. I approached the foreman. He was a giant with big shoulders, a big mouth full of big teeth, and a big laugh. "Good day. I painted all morning long, and I was wondering if there is another job I can do this afternoon."

He listened to what I said. *Hmmmmed* and *hawwwwwed*. He was thinking. He looked around the job site and said, "You can pick up all the trash."

He didn't get it. I said, "I have as much experience as the men on my team: none. I didn't travel over seven thousand miles to pick up trash. I want to build a house for those five children." I pointed to the little girls who were now looking at me.

He let out a big guffaw. The other builders nearby stopped and watched. "I forgot you're an American woman. Get on the roof. And be careful not to nail your knee to it."

I immediately wondered if I had enough insurance to cover a knee nailed to the roof. What would it feel like? How would they get the nail out? If I passed out, would it rip the nail out when I fell off the roof, or would the nail stay put and save me from falling?

Then I thought of all the fun the boys had had that I'd missed out on when I was told I should be afraid of getting hurt. When I was told to be careful. When I was sent to the Girls' Field. I was done watching. I was done shrinking. I was done staying in place.

I was holding my breath. I let it out. I breathed in deeply and replied, "I can do that!" He pointed to the ladder.

I put on my tool belt, strutted over to the ladder, and climbed up one rung at a time. The view was breathtaking; I saw all the workers building, the children running around watching their new homes being built, and the women painting, painting, painting over in the corner.

I was assigned to Kurt. He checked me out as a member of his crew, not a prospect, and lifted his sunglasses so I could see his eyes. "You won't nail your knee, mate." We both smiled.

He gave me the directions on how to not nail my knee to the roof and handed me a nail gun that was about half my body weight. The first time I used it, I shot back three feet. I looked around—nobody had seemed to notice. They were too busy building the house for the families. I stumbled and gained my footing. I checked the nail; it was in the wood and not my knee. And it was straight. Kurt and I looked at each other and smiled; I could do this.

Before I knew it, it was teatime. Cookies. This time, I was sweating, and when I climbed down the ladder, my team was waiting for me. "How was it?" "How did you do?" "What did you do up there with all those men?" I shared how beautiful it was to see everybody working together as a collective. Three on my team listened intently. "I'm afraid of heights," Cathy said. Joe and Stacy nodded their heads in agreement.

I leaned in closely. "I am too." Sweaty and exhausted, I got back on the roof.

After a bit, I heard, "Kristi! Kristi!" I looked around for the voices; it was my three teammates who'd confided they were afraid of heights too. They were on the roof next to me, waving and giving me thumbs-ups!

A film crew came by to capture the good work we were doing—and of course they chose the American woman on the roof with the nail gun. I waved with one hand and hefted my nail gun in the other.

Later, the foreman grunted at me and pointed to the soffits. I leaned over the house and nailed the soffit to the roof. I teetered gracefully on the edge of the house as my team leader Kurt watched from afar. I was improving, but nobody wanted to stand under me while I shot nails into an unknown space. Good idea.

At the turn of the millennium, I showed the foreman, my American team, and the little girls who would share the room I helped build that women belong where men are. We are brave. We can learn just as quickly as men. We don't belong in the corner. And you want us on the roof with you.

———

Two decades later, I still notice the gaps, and I still say something because I know little girls are watching. And others are watching too: women who want to climb the Eagle's Nest, men who can challenge the way things have always been done, and boys who see how strong, brave, and powerful women are.

And I'm still getting on the roof: clay tiles in India, metal sheets of zinc in Thailand, and asphalt tiles in South Dakota. Because once I got on the roof—a woman who wears big hoop earrings, has no building experience, and is still afraid of heights—others followed.

Sometimes you need to be first, so others can see what they can be.

HOW TO GET ON THE ROOF.

1. **Take up space.** Believe you belong on the roof and get up there. I practice affirmations. One of my favorites is "I belong . . . on the national stage, at the UN, in the same room with Melinda Gates." Now, stand in your space. If you're having trouble seeing yourself on the roof, look for other women who are already doing it and reach out to them. I reached out to Dr. Lois Frankel, author of *Nice Girls Don't Get the Corner Office*, to ask if I could interview her about her changemaking journey, and she responded the same day with, "Yes." Where do you belong?

2. **Be first.** Be the first to see the view from the top. The top of Mt. Kilimanjaro, the top of the corporate ladder, the top of

your passion. If you can't do it for yourself, do it for me. But seriously, if you're struggling to do something just for you, then do it for your daughter. For other women and girls watching. For the doubters. Be first, even when you're afraid, so others can see what they can be. Where will you be first?

3. Look for the helpers. Pay attention to who is supporting you quietly and loudly. And then let them. Kurt (and the crew) gave me a safe space to succeed and fail. He gave me the tools (acumen) to succeed, and then let me do it. And I like to believe the foreman saw and felt the sense of team I was creating and saw my potential to do a more difficult job with the soffits. Cathy, Joe, and Stacy were allies too; they cheered me on and then followed. When you have doubts, who will you reach out to?

NOW, GET ON THAT ROOF!

IT'S OK; YOU DON'T HAVE TO GET MARRIED.

I have yet to hear a man ask for advice on how to combine marriage and a career.

—GLORIA STEINEM

SUMMER 2020.

I get a text from my niece. "I have a semi-loaded question."

I texted back, "Are you safe?"

"Yes. Thank you for asking."

"I'm ready," I replied.

For me, the role of Auntie Kristi is the ultimate sponsor. I'm here to listen, to share wisdom, and to love, love, love. Although I have only one full biological niece and three acquired nieces, I'm an auntie to hundreds of young women and girls around the world.

"OK, so like first of all yeah. I'm 19 and obviously have years before any of this is a real topic or concern but this has been in my head since last week, and I really think you understand better than most. I have NEVER EVER EVER wanted children. And I've also never been too keen on the idea of getting married. Like never. Marriage seems scary."

The texts kept coming.

"Anytime the topic ever comes up, I hear, 'Oh, you'll change your mind!' But I don't think I will. I feel like there's so much

women to choose between having a really success-
ıd personal life and having a family. To be honest,
e two I'd pick the first without a doubt, and ever
ıown you, I've always really admired you as a person
hink you have such a good heart and strong personality.

"And this is honestly none of my business, so forgive me, but do you ever regret not doing the whole marriage and kids thing? And how did/do you deal with people pressuring you to have kids and get married?"

I was relieved. This felt easy compared to other texts I'd received from young women over the years about not wanting to live anymore, not wanting to eat anymore, or fearing this time he was going to kill her. I responded. "First, I'm honored you reached out to me. Second, I am with you. I never saw myself getting married or having children. Children are one of my favorite things in the world, and I've built a life around them (especially girls), but I don't want the lifestyle. And yes, I would have been a kick-bum mom, but I'm an awesome auntie. I feel like my role in the world is to give love where it's needed, and where I can. There's plenty of opportunities to do that. No regrets."

I added, "I don't usually get pressure because of what you call my 'strong personality,' which tells me that people DO know that what they're asking is not helpful and is judgmental. I have a story I wrote for my friend Haley. Do you want me to send it?"

"Yeah."

DECEMBER 2015.

"I've scoured the bookshelves for somebody to tell me it's OK to not want to get married and have babies. It's OK to want to live a life I want. It's OK to not belong to somebody else." Haley splayed her body across the table in defeat. "Kristi, you need to write it."

I was shocked. Haley is one of the few other women I've come across that has self-assurance as one of her innate strengths.[1] She had just been hired by Facebook, had been chosen by Steve Case to present her idea on a big stage, had made the first cut in a national start-up competition, already had a TED Talk under her belt, and wanted *me* to tell her it was OK?

I struggled with this because I teach women that waiting for permission is giving your power away. Haley didn't need permission to be fierce, brilliant, nor confident. What was this about? Why me?

I was in my late forties and for the first time in my life had a boyfriend. I'd been to sixty-five countries and lived out of a backpack for a total of six years of my life on twenty dollars a day.

"How did you do it?" Haley asked.

"What do you mean?" I replied.

"How did you deal with the pressure? The questions? The judgment?"

Haley was folded over. Exhausted. Her face was sullen. I wanted to lean over and give her a hug, but that's not what she needed. She needed me to put it in words.

"After Michael and I holiday on Condado Beach in Puerto Rico, I have a week at a hostel in Old San Juan. I will write something for you," I promised.

PUERTO RICO, 2015.

After our five days at a fancy ocean suite in Condado, Puerto Rico, my boyfriend flew back to Minneapolis to work, and I

1   Strengthfinders 2.0. https://www.gallup.com/cliftonstrengths/

transferred to my four-bed, all-girl-dorm-room, seventeen-dollars-a-night hostel for an additional week in Old San Juan. I have found that when I travel solo, I learn a lot more about the location, people, and myself.

Please don't let me get a top bunk. Please don't let me get a top bunk, I chanted in my head as I lugged my suitcase up six flights of stairs in the ninety-degree weather. What was an adventure when I was in my teens was now a punishment in my forties; the rungs on the ladder hurt my feet, and without my contacts in it was hard to see the ladder. I got the top bunk.

As I pouted on the top bunk, thinking about the infinity pool I'd just left, a dirty-blonde girl clad in a clichéd Panama hat stormed into the room, looked up at her bunk, and said, "I'm too old for a top bunk. And it's my birthday." I giggled; we became best friends on our top bunks, swapping life stories. I learned Mindy had a baby named Jack she hadn't planned for and a divorce from a husband she didn't want. She missed her travels and life "before Jack."

Mindy felt guilty for not missing Jack. She felt guilty she was in a safe job that allowed her to give Jack a ride to school in the morning and pick him up. She shared her dream of working in hospice one day when she could afford it. Distraught, Mindy decided to abandon the "top bunk" life and splurge on a $160 room at a hotel so she could do some soul searching. She left me with our two other roomies—each of whom had a bottom bunk and was probably in her twenties.

The next day, she texted me that she had been up for hours pooing. I brought Gatorade to her fancy-schmancy inn and stayed to make sure she felt better. "Maybe I don't have the flu," Mindy said. "Maybe I don't have food poisoning or IBS. Maybe I'm purging the crap in my life?" She described the countless women she saw as a nurse who used their health as an excuse to escape from their miserable lives. "Have I become them?"

I sent Mindy off into the sunset of poo and existential questions and rushed off to meet the twentysomethings who had the bottom bunks for happy hour.

Megan and Emily were forest firefighters who lived in Colorado and were sent to the wildfires we see on television—but only from April to October, when the fires rage. When not fighting forest fires, they traveled around the world.

I changed into a dress and heels and even put on my signature hot-pink lipstick. "How did you fit a pair of heels in that bag?" Megan asked.

"Always pack something you can interview in, something you can attend a gala in, and something you can salsa in," I said.

Emily and Megan laughed. "We have a lot to learn from you," said Megan.

"Traveling the world, listening to my ambition, and being true to Little Kristi's dreams have taught me a lot. And I'm still learning," I replied.

We headed to the rooftop for four-dollar sangria happy hour. Megan told me about her iguana hunt from the day before and how Emily had got the big one. "There was this one that I didn't hit just right . . ."

"This is the part you shouldn't tell Kristi," Emily interjected. She shifted in her seat and leaned in. "Why is it that boyfriends don't understand that as a forest firefighter, I am on twenty-four seven during the season? That I can't just hop in a car and be there? And so we break up."

We made a pact over sangrias that society's expectations wouldn't be the barrier to our success. We were not damn Cinderellas; we would create our own happy endings.

"And why do the women who are now in leadership positions at the firehouse ignore me and make things worse?" Megan added.

We made another pact: we wouldn't be the barrier to another woman's success. We would bring other women along in our success.

The next day, the girls headed back to Colorado, and I snagged a bottom bunk. Dani and I were the only ones in the room. As we sat alone in the room, she asked, "What are you doing for dinner? I don't like to eat alone or go out alone."

"What made you come on this trip alone, then?" I asked.

"I'm graduating from Columbia University at the end of the month and going back to China." For the next thirty minutes, I listened to Dani describe her time in NYC, the rough adjustment to American life, her boyfriend waiting for her return after her degree in construction management, and her parents telling her, "Do not push yourself too hard; you don't need to do big things. You have us and your boyfriend here. Come back to China."

Dani's warmth and directness were refreshing. In her sure-fire, staccato way, she asked, "What if I regret it? What if I'm missing opportunities in the States? What if I do want to push myself and do big things? When I'm old, will I wonder about what I could be doing instead?"

"Your boyfriend is an architect. Would he join you in the States?" I asked.

Sigh. "If I don't come back, we will end." Dani didn't look sad. She didn't look lost. Her dislike of being alone felt like a limiting belief; she enjoyed herself. Loved herself. She was stronger than she thought.

I ended up going for tapas with Dani on the rooftop. I headed back early to read and journal, and she stayed with our Swedish roomie Anna and an American guy staying at our hostel.

I met our next roomie, Eve. Eve was a New Yorker. She appeared bold, self-assured, and unafraid. She was living in La Ceiba, Honduras, doing impactful work with the locals.

She told me that she had just nailed an interview for her dream job in Seattle, but her boyfriend was studying medicine in Guatemala. She wasn't sure what to do.

"How is this your dream job?" I asked.

"It will make BIG impact, it pays well, and it's where I want to be," she fired back.

"Why would you say no to that?"

"I'm not sure he will allow me to do both."

"Both?" I questioned.

"Be his girlfriend and work in Seattle," Eve replied.

"How will you decide what to do?" I wondered.

"I'm not sure."

She flopped on her bed and put her eye mask on. As I worked on this story, Dani came back, stuck her earplugs in, and passed out on her bed. I finished up my work and turned the lights out.

I woke up to hear a man and a woman arguing outside our dorm room. I knew the sound. Anger. Our Swedish roomie Anna stormed into the room and huffed up to her bed. The guy pounded on the door. She yelled for him to stop. He continued. She climbed back down the ladder and stepped outside.

I couldn't hear the words, but I could tell he was agitated. She snuck back into the room, slammed the door, and locked it, then climbed back into bed.

"Sorry," she whispered.

"You should be for waking us up," said Eve.

"Are you OK?" I asked. No answer.

I was on red alert. The pounding continued. It grew louder. A neighboring guy heard it, stepped outside, and argued with the guy about leaving us alone. The voices grew more agitated and the pounding rattled the door. I looked for escapes. There was a tiny window that dropped off the fourth floor.

"Do you think we need to call the police?" I asked Anna.

"I'm getting the number now," said Eve. She screamed into the night, "We're calling the police! I have the number right here. I'm ready to dial it."

"If you pound the door one more time, we're calling the police," I added with authority and experience.

I knew the type from my work in domestic violence. The pounding stopped. The others fell asleep; I waited another twenty minutes before I started to relax.

I awoke early to write; it's my travel routine learned from all those years of sharing rooms with others. When I returned, Eve and Dani were gone. Anna came back from the shower. "I want to apologize for last night," she began. "I don't know what happened. He was an OK guy when we were drinking; he said nice things and told me about his success in America. He said he'd walk me home since we were staying at the same hostel. He followed me to my room, and when I said good night, he freaked out. He couldn't believe I didn't want to hook up with him; he couldn't accept I didn't want to be with him. I'm not that kind of girl, you know." She looked down at her feet.

"Are you in danger now?" I asked.

"No. I found out he checked out, and I'm going to check out also. I'm so ashamed."

"What are you ashamed about?" I asked.

"That he woke you up, and I drank too much," she said.

"He was the one pounding down the door," I added. She smiled.

———

I think back to my five days in the hostel, Haley's desperate questions, and my niece's painful text. No wonder young women are struggling.

I think about how my role as auntie (sponsor, ally, advocate, mentor) is even more important than I imagined.

So here it is; the validation you've been craving. You are lovable without a partner. You have value without children. In fact, a recent headline in *Business Insider* read, "Women who are unmarried and childless are the happiest people of all."

Paul Dolan, a professor of behavioral science at the London School of Economics, says that while men benefit from being married, women generally don't. Although tying the knot and having children are typically considered markers of success in our society, women who shun this pressure, despite the stigma, tend to be happier and healthier as a result.[2]

There. You have proof now.

But really, living the life you want is about knowing yourself and valuing what you want—no matter what anybody says or thinks. It's about choosing. To get married, or not. To have children, or not. Owning your power.

It's OK to get married. It's OK to not get married. It's OK to have children. It's OK to not want children. Ultimately, it's OK to be you.

But *really*, Haley, my beloved niece, and all of you nodding your head right now, you didn't need to hear that from me. You knew it all along. Believe in you.

HOW TO BE "OK."

1. **Take up space.** Let your dreams take up space. Your business. Your innovation. Your name. Don't change your name if you don't want to—or have your partner take on your name. And when you need it, here it is: "It's OK to be you." Take out a sticky note or your phone and write, "It's OK to _____." What would you write on the line?

2. **Be first.** To not get married. To not have children. To create your own definition of "family." I was talking to my friend who is in her late fifties about this phenomenon, and she said

2   Oppenheim, Maya. "Women who are unmarried and childless are the happiest people of all, according to a professor of behavioral science." *Business Insider.* http://static1.businessinsider.com/unmarried-childless-women-are-happiest-expert-says-2019-5

that it feels like it's more OK to not get married than to not have children. The childless woman is the bottom of the hierarchy. She said that often women will whisper to her, "I'm sorry that you and your husband couldn't have children." Or she gets a cheerful, happy, "Why don't you adopt?" Nobody seems to hear, "We don't want children."

As you read above, I never saw myself in a white dress getting married. I didn't see children for myself. However, I'm an educator; you don't go around broadcasting that you don't want children when all day long you work with other women's children. When I told one mom I didn't want the lifestyle, she told me, "You probably shouldn't tell other moms this, or they won't want their children in your classroom." I replied, "Moms should want me. The teachers who are moms are thinking of their own children all the time. Not yours. I only have yours on my mind." I smiled my Blessed Southern Smile, and she shut up.

What do you see for you?

3. Look for the helpers. Look for your aunties. I am president of my company. I am an author. I am a world traveler. I am a social entrepreneur. And my favorite title is auntie. When I was living in Japan, I became fast friends with Intern Aya. She affectionately called me Oneechan (big sister in Japanese), and I called her Imouto (little sister). But really, with our age difference, I was an auntie. I was there to share my wisdom and experience; she was there to remind me to play and embrace what's possible. We learned from each other—without all the family dysfunction. Who is the "auntie" (sponsor, ally, advocate, mentor) you can turn to for support?

NOW, GO FIND YOUR "AUNTIE." AND IF YOU HAVE A FAVORITE ONE ALREADY, GO THANK HER! WE AUNTIES LOVE WHAT WE DO, BUT THERE IS NO AUNTIE DAY. YET.

WOMAN UP; MAN DOWN?

*The first problem for all of us, men and
women, is not to learn, but to unlearn.*

—GLORIA STEINEM

BALI, 2018.

I wore my *Woman Up* shirt on my first morning walk on Sanur
Beach in Bali. Every year I take a MEtreat to Bali to get away
from the tundra of the Midwest and to just be. The shirt always gets looks and comments, especially in Bali, where women
rarely walk alone on the beach or have a coffee solo. On my way
to my favorite coffee shop, I headed down the alley, where a
gaggle of taxi drivers asked the obligatory question: "Transport?"

My automatic response was, "*Tidak* [no, thank you]."

And then, the drivers together sounded out the English
words on my T-shirt, "W-o-m-a-n Up."

PAUSE.

"Man Down?" they wondered aloud.

I laughed. This was the same response I'd gotten the last year
when I wore this shirt. "No, not Man Down. Woman Up. Man
Up."

When I got to the coffee shop, I ordered an iced drink. I noticed on the clear plastic cup that *MRS.* was written in black
sharpie. Hmmm. Everybody assumed at my age, I was married.

Heck, in Bali, if you were half my age and female, you were married.

In fact, when I lived in Indonesia in 2001 as an international educator, I was taught in my cultural class that if an Indonesian asked if you were married, the polite (and only) response if single was, "*Belum* [not yet]."

I noticed that below *MRS.* on my cup, it said, *I like your outfit today.*

I liked my outfit too. I wore a black skort with my black-and-white *Woman Up* shirt hanging off my shoulder like the '80s. My fashionista friend Jenn asked how I got an off-the-shoulder shirt now. I told her I'd bought it two sizes too big. It hung off my shoulder like Madonna and Belinda Carlisle.

HOUSTON, 1997.

I love chocolate. Everybody at the private middle school I was teaching sixth-grade humanities at knew this. I went into the faculty lounge, and there was a pan of brownies. One was left.

I looked at it. I admired it. I circled it. I drooled over it. But I didn't take it. I had been taught, "It's not nice to take the last one."

Thomas, our finance officer, meandered to the pan, picked it up, and before he popped it into his mouth said, "When you know your value, you eat the last brownie." He looked at me, ate the brownie in one bite, brushed the crumbs off his face, and headed back to his office.

Thomas valued me as a teacher. He valued me as a woman. He valued me as a leader. He wanted me not only to value myself (which I did) but also to show my value to the world (which I didn't). To let others know that I knew my value. That I was worth the last brownie.

Since then, I have practiced the "Last Brownie Mindset" to

take the last dollars for professional development, the last seat at the table, the last promotion of the review cycle, the last seat on the bus.

It was not about being first or last; it was about caring enough about myself to know what I wanted and believe I was worth it. Because over and over and over again, I saw women hovering over the last brownie, the last promotion, the last seat on the conference call, the last spot on stage to present. I shared the "Last Brownie Mindset" with them in hopes that they too would see their value, know what they wanted, and take it—without even thinking about how many calories were in it.

DUBUQUE, 2014.

"Hemmer, I called four women to suggest they apply for the leadership position, and nobody would," said my friend from high school and college. His candor and real concern gave me hope for the world.

"Why is this a problem?" I asked. I had my own ideas, but I wanted to hear his.

"I need my top talent to stay. These women are my top talent and are not acting like it. I'm a dad of three girls; I want them to have the same opportunity as men. And I'm a husband who sees his wife not go after leadership positions she's not only qualified for but is the best person for."

I too felt his pain. I heard one of my best teacher friends share the gaps in her school and her innovative ideas to solve them, yet she didn't apply for the principal position that would give her the power to close that gap. She told me, "I'm friends with all the teachers; I don't want that to change."

An old student of mine who was now all grown up told me that she was really interested in a position but didn't have the five years' experience that was listed. She had four-and-a-half years. And when we really dug deep, we realized that nobody in her company had more experience than her.

And I remember my client sharing that she was told she couldn't apply for a directorial position because she hadn't been a manager yet. She didn't apply. The person who was hired also did not have a managerial position; he was a man.

"I can help you with that," I replied to Mark. I didn't know how when I told Mark that, but I knew I would figure it out.

From this interaction, I designed a systems-approached changemaking course with a cohort that focuses on women's potential and their systems: the manager (who is usually a man the first time through, but not afterward), the senior leaders (again, usually men), and the company as a whole come together on a group project to create change.

It is modeled on sponsorship vs. mentorship. To me, sponsorship is what I call an Equitable Energy Exchange™. It's not a traditional, one-way relationship of the senior leader telling or advising the junior leader; it's both ways. For example, my intern was able to learn about the intersection of feminism and capitalism, experience running a social business, and have a safe space to lead while interning with me. In sponsorship style, she thought the workshops I did with corporate women on owning your power were needed at her university; she connected me with her professor, who agreed and hired me to teach a workshop on presence. In addition, my intern introduced me to the alum group, and they hired me to do a workshop on sponsorship. Sponsorship isn't equal—it's equitable. Value and connection are exchanged. When she moved to DC, I connected her with my friends who lived there to help her adjust and to sponsor her.

Sponsorship has been called the "Great Equalizer" by Sylvia Ann Hewlett in her book *The Sponsor Effect*.[1] I agree. I believe

1   Hewlett, Sylvia Ann. *The Sponsor Effect: How to Be a Better Leader by Investing in Others*. Boston: Harvard Business Press, 2019.

sponsorship is not only the "Great Equalizer" for gender but also for race, age, ableism, LGBTQ issues, and other areas that are not equal.

MINNEAPOLIS, EQUALITY DAY 2019.

After hearing story after story of men who thought they were doing better for their daughters, partners, and colleagues and were not, I wanted to give men a safe space to show up to ask questions, to share stories, and to learn what to do.

The idea of doing a men-only event came from the men themselves. "I've been told I don't know how to talk to women right. What do I do?" "Women on our team keep leaving. What do I do?" "My wife isn't going for the promotion. What do I do?" "I'm afraid for my daughter's safety on the college campus. What do I do?"

While I was creating the Equality Day event for just men, I was asked by a trusted, white, cisgender, male friend, "Why would I want anything to change, Kristi? I'm doing just fine." And then he asked, "Why would I or any other man show up to this?"

To answer these candid and valuable questions, I created a focus group of men and asked why they *would* show up. I also created a focus group of women, asking what they wished men knew. Finally, I recruited a powerful panel and intern to set us up for success.

I thought it would be a sold-out event with a waiting list. That was Kristi's World. In reality, I ended up recruiting ten men with the promise of a free lunch and golf afterward. The women ambassadors from my focus group who had great influence and power at their companies recruited ZERO men. The men they talked to said, "It sounds interesting." And then nothing.

For those who did show up, their vulnerability, candor, and

engagement were impressive. The event was a success not only because of the deep conversations but also because of the impact. In response to my follow-up email a month later, one said it improved his marriage because he listened better and asked powerful questions to understand, one said it improved his understanding of his daughter, and another asked, "When are we doing the next one?"

Girls and boys, women and men are set up in a win-lose binary system. If I'm popular, you can't be. If I win, you must lose. If I have equal rights, you can't.

And I have found that women are often the first to take the "lose" card. "Go ahead, you eat the last brownie; I'm on a diet anyhow." "You'll get the promotion this time, and I'll wait until next time."

I encourage women (and men) to "middle think." What is in the space between? Opportunities, possibilities for innovations, and even negotiations. I read Stephen Covey's *The 7 Habits of Highly Effective People* when I was twenty-two, and it changed my life. As a competitive person, I had some deep learning to do with Habit 4: "Think Win-Win."

Now, I focus on what I call win-win-win thinking. How can I win? And you win? AND how can the collective good or humanity win too? I get the promotion, and I bring you along with me, and that models to the company and team that there is enough for everybody. A Growth Mindset v. a Fixed Mindset.

When a woman is more confident, she will live to her potential and have a job that pays her what's she worth. This takes off some of the pressure for the man to be the provider, which will give him headspace to be more present with the children. Collectively, the family will model a new way of being.

When a man is more emotionally equipped, he is able to show emotions other than anger, and when he's angry, he's able to process it without violence. This will create a safer space for the woman and the family and will break the cycle of violence and stop it from spreading to future generations. In addition, he can be a role model for other men and a change agent for speaking up in his system.

Think of the last time you "won." How could you make it into a "win" for the other and for the collective whole? What would be different?

HOW TO WIN-WIN-WIN.

1. Take up space. Eat the last damn brownie! Know your value. And if you don't know, find out. Ask other women and men how much money they are making and even ask how much money they think you should be making. If you're uncomfortable asking people you work with, go to www.fairygodboss.com and ask the community; it's the place for "Jobs. Advice. Connections."

Ask recruiters. Search the internet. Websites like Salary.com, the US Bureau of Labor Statistics, Glassdoor, and Indeed can give you a starting point. And practice the Last Brownie Mindset, where you know your value, believe it, and show it to the world. What is the first step to understanding your value?

2. Be first. To bust echo chambers. Surround yourself not only with different genders, but with different races, different religions, different political views, different industries, different ages, different strengths, and people from different places. Urban and rural. South Dakota and New York. Indonesia and Nicaragua. When I set up my advisory team for AWE, I intentionally chose different perspectives, experiences, and strengths because I already had an echo chamber in my head; I didn't want another one to advise me. Who do you need in your circle to bust up your echoing chamber?

3. Look for the helpers. Seek out sponsors—those who are willing to take risks for you and see your value. As Sallie

Krawcheck said in *Own It: The Power of Women at Work*, a sponsor is somebody who speaks up for you when you're not in the room. And make sure that person is really a sponsor. I was working with a client, Melanie, who was pushing back on an idea that would cost the company millions in loss; she felt strongly enough to risk her job. I asked her, "Who is speaking up for you when you're not in the room?" She responded immediately with, "Ginny." I asked, "Does Ginny know this?" Pause. Melanie went back and confirmed with Ginny that she indeed would speak up for her. Who is speaking up for you when you're not in the room?

NOW GO WOMAN AND MAN UP.

MEAN GIRLS: QUIT BEING SO GOOD REPRISE.

When humans are ranked instead of linked, everyone loses.

—GLORIA STEINEM

MINNEAPOLIS, OCTOBER 2019.

"This ferociously funny stage adaption infuses the iconic comedy with energetic music and dance while examining tribalism, community and what it means to characters who explore hierarchies and ask the ever present question: Where do you belong?" *—Mark Nerenhausen,* Mean Girls *review,* Playbill

"What made you say yes to going to *Mean Girls: The Musical* with me?" I asked my boyfriend Michael.

"I watched the trailer," he replied quickly.

"Did you think it was funny?" I asked.

"No. I thought of you and the pain you go through."

Gulp. He felt my pain of being an "overachiever." "Type A." A social entrepreneur. Somebody who was told over and over and over again, "Quit being so good." "Not yet." "You're doing too much." "You're liked too much." "You're making me look bad."

Just last week on the phone a family member said to me, "I

don't know if I should tell you this, because it could give you a bigger head, but my friend said she thinks you're beautiful."

I've gained weight. I'm perimenopausal. I have a lot of facial hair. My hair is thinning. I need to wear readers. I'm not able to run a 5k anymore. I can pinch more than an inch. I don't feel beautiful.

Instead of feeling better, I felt like I'd been punched in the gut. I wondered, *Why wouldn't she want to tell me? When people share nice things about her, I can't wait to tell her. Why would she not want me to feel better, stronger? Why would she want to hurt me?* Silence. What do you say to that?

"Well, it's not normal to have that much energy. To get so much done. To do so much," she added.

I felt the awkwardness between us build. *Quit Being So Good.* Quit being you. You don't belong.

I was holding my breath. I reminded myself of what my therapist said: "Deep breaths." Three seconds in. Six seconds out.

"I have to get ready for my next meeting; I better go," she said.

We hung up the phone. I messaged my therapist and scheduled an appointment.

THE DELTA, 2005.

I was a principal in an all-girls school in the deep South. I drove a fancy car, belonged to a country club, and lived in a custom-made new house, and I was miserable.

My boss, who was my mentor for almost a decade, recruited me hard for three years before I said yes to coming to her school to be the boss. When I was interviewing, I asked her, "What do you want most from this position?"

"An instructional leader," she responded straight away.

I didn't have my master's in administration, but I was a damn good instructional leader. I could do that!

At the end of year one, I was scheduled for my annual review, where rumor had it that I would be told whether I got a raise or even still had a job. I was anxious because one of the other directors had just been told in her review that she was lucky to still have a job and was not going to get a raise. She was on an "action plan." I was also anxious—I had no idea what my boss thought of how I was doing other than the "Good job" I got when I met with her monthly. Like most women, I was not given any critical feedback; according to *Forbes*, women are less likely to receive specific feedback tied to the outcomes of their work.

I was in my boss's spacious office, sitting on a chair upholstered with happy yellow fabric sprayed with daisies. Around me were matching wallpaper and carpeting, massive bookshelves with books about empowering girls, and floor-to-ceiling windows overlooking the pond. I reminded myself of what I'd learned in my counseling degree: "Be the non-anxious presence." *I am prepared for an unpreparable meeting. I could be fired. I could be promoted. Hell, I could have a building named after me. With her, you never knew.*

My boss said, "You're too good of a teacher. The teachers are intimidated by you."

But you wanted an Instructional Leader, I said in my head.

"The girls love you too much; the teachers are jealous of you," my boss continued.

I know all their names. I'm not giving that up, I argued silently.

I was holding my breath. I thought, *I'm going to be fired for being too good. I will look like a failure. Kristi Hemmer cannot fail.* And then relief spread; I didn't want to work here anymore.

"You're not vulnerable enough; you need to show emotion. But we can work on that. You're getting a three-percent raise."

There was a knock at the door; on cue, her executive assistant said, "Your next appointment is here." The review was over, but it was far from over for me.

I found out from Laura, one of the few teachers who didn't want to see me fail, what was meant by "vulnerable." The challenge in the faculty lounge was called "Who can make Kristi cry?" Teachers o. Me 1. It didn't feel like a win.

So when *Mean Girls* the movie came out and Laura asked, "Are you going to see *Mean Girls*?" I replied, "Why would I? I live it every day."

She nodded her head knowingly, shut my office door, approached my desk. "My daughters go here. I've taught here for twelve years. And I still don't belong. You're not alone, Kristi."

Damn. It was my ally who was going to make me cry. Graciously, she left before the tears dropped.

Quit Being So Good. Quit being you. You don't belong.

It wasn't about fitting into the elitist crowd for Laura. There were enough zeros in Laura's husband's salary, she drove the right minivan, and she belonged to the right clubs, but she was one of my strongest teachers. In a private, elite school where teachers took out mimeographs from twenty years ago for the girls to color within the lines after being given a Dum Dum for doing their homework, she was too good too.

SHOWTIME, 2019.

Over a decade later, I was finally able to go to *Mean Girls*, but I still felt anxious. I didn't really want to see it, but this time, I wasn't alone. I was with my boyfriend, and I purposely bought seats at the very back of the auditorium where I could hide or exit quickly if I needed to. Even as the founder and president of Academy for Women's Empowerment, I worried that the show would cause a lot of the scars from Little Kristi and Grown-Up Kristi to resurface. *Quit Being So Good.*

Even while I was writing this book, my friend who I was meeting for an event at 9:00 a.m. texted me. When I told her I was at Starbucks working, she said, "Overachiever!"

Quit Being So Good. This was from somebody who was a local celebrity, ran several companies, maintained two residences, and was working on her second book.

I don't call her an overachiever; I call her an inspiration.

NOW.

I reflect back to the review by the man. "This ferociously funny stage adaption infuses the iconic comedy with energetic music and dance while examining tribalism, community and what it means to characters who explore hierarchies and ask the ever present question: Where do you belong?"

Mean Girls is not a comedy.

Mean Girls is a timeless story of growing up as a girl that explores what it means to belong, compete, grow into who you really are, and choose to thrive together or survive alone. In real life, we know there isn't a happy ending. In real life, when you choose to be "unapologetically you," you are the happy ending.

So why are girls and women mean to each other? I get asked that a lot. To me, it's not about the scarcity of seats at the table for women; it's about belonging. When there is a safe space where you feel included and show up as your powerful, good self even if it risks hurting somebody's feelings, you will feel confident, purposeful, and part of a community. Then you can bring others along in your success.

And the research concurs. The *Harvard Business Review* says that belonging is "being accepted and included by those around you" and is good for business and workers. When workers feel like they belong, there is a 50 percent drop in turnover risk, a 75 percent drop in sick days, raises are doubled, and there are eighteen times as many promotions.[1]

---

1   Carr, Evan W., Andrew Reece, Gabriella Rosen Kellerman, and Alexi Robichaux. "The Value of Belonging at Work." *Harvard Business Review.* https://hbr.org/2019/12/the-value-of-belonging-at-work

To me, not feeling safe is the root of workplace exclusion. It's the root of loneliness. It's the root of Mean Girls. Looking back, it's no surprise that I didn't feel like I belonged. The school was not a safe place. Decisions were reversed. Promises were made and then broken. Secrets were standard practice. Public shame was common. It wasn't competition (nobody else wanted my job), it was exclusion. Loneliness. Fear. And shaming for being too good. For not fitting in.

In addition to finding a safe space where you feel like you belong, I encourage you to create your own safe space to retreat to. For me, it's writing. I started writing in a diary when I was eleven and have journaled since. It is my safe space of belonging to my thoughts, my ideas, my beliefs. It's where I remind myself to keep going; to believe in my goal of changing one million lives and making one million dollars, unapologetically; and to MOXIEon. It's my anchor. What is your safe space?

It's time to own your story. To write your own review. To create safe spaces. To accept yourself and your power. To take up space, unapologetically. To belong. Because the world needs you.

HOW TO BELONG.

1. **Take up space.** Own your story. When I was talking to a high school class, a girl asked me, "Kristi, what's your muse?" I asked her, "What do you think it is?" She said, "To serve others." I replied, "It's not to serve others but to spread MOXIE and create a safer and more equitable world for you and other girls in the class."

One of my favorite thought leaders said in a blog that businesses should "serve others' needs to be first." Easy to say for this man who his whole life has only been expected to serve himself. Now, he's going to look at serving others after he's made a name and fortune for himself. Bullshit. To me, it's not about serving others. I'm not on this earth to serve you. I'm on this earth to make the world safer and more equitable for women. To make change. To disrupt. To inspire. Not to serve. I've spent enough years serving into the system of women caretaking and men taking. I'm taking up the space I need to create systemic change. What is your muse?

2. Be first. Create a safe space for yourself. And then others. One way to do both is allyship. Thankfully, research shows that if you have just one ally who treats you equally (not specially), exclusion can be fixed. Don't only identify allies for yourself; show up as an ally for others—especially for those who may not look, act, or believe as you do. For example, I know that my friend and I would love to go to a workshop offered at a local women's co-working space. I also know that most of those who attend will be white women; she is Black. I invite her, show up early, and save her a seat, so even if she's the only Black woman, she will have a safe space right next to me. What do you need to feel safe?

3. Look for the helpers. Who makes you feel safe? Who makes you feel included? Find leaders, companies, and a circle of influence that includes, not excludes. I have my educator friends, I have my international friends, I have my travel friends, and I have my entrepreneur friends. For me right now, I'm building a group of authors to help me feel safe in the writing world. To help me navigate contracts, intellectual property, and negative feedback. Right now, where don't you feel safe? What do you need to feel safe? Who can help?

NOW, CREATE A SPACE WHERE YOU BELONG (AND OTHERS TOO).

LIVING ON TWENTY DOLLARS A DAY.

*When people ask me why I still have hope and energy
after all these years, I always say: Because I travel.*

—GLORIA STEINEM

DUBUQUE, IOWA, 1986.

Freud's *The Interpretation of Dreams* fascinated me my junior
year in high school. In psychology class, we'd share our reoccurring dreams. Then my teacher would look in his large manual
to find the dream and tell us what it meant. I raised my hand.
"My reoccurring dream is that I'm being chased by dogs." Which
made sense to me because I was deathly afraid of dogs.

Mr. B. thumbed through the manual. "Hmmmm. It means
you're looking for love."

There were giggles, ooohs, and aaahs, and then my classmate
Randy asked, "Are you looking for me?" I laughed it off. Looking
back, I wasn't looking for a romance kind of love; I was search-
ing for self-love.

In the same class, we learned about Maslow's hierarchy of
needs. I'm competitive. I love to win. And winning in life, according to Maslow, is self-actualization. My teacher said,
"Maybe one of us in here will get to be self-actualized."

It will be me, I said. Silently, of course. I wasn't about to be
interpreted again.

TOKYO, SEPTEMBER 2009.

Here I was again. In a place that was toxic. Another school teaching not only girls but me to: "Quit Being So Good." *When will I learn? Right now.* It was time to leave.

I searched for openings for the next school year. There was a position for the dean of a middle school open in Bangkok. I did some research on the school, found who I knew that worked there, reached out to them, figured out what my value-add was, and updated my resume, but when I sat down to write my cover letter about why I wanted to work there, I drew a blank.

Bangkok has beaches. Bangkok is innovative, with one of the first social businesses in the world, a restaurant called Cabbages and Condoms. Their slogan is, "Our food is guaranteed not to cause pregnancy." The founder, Mechai Viravaidya, helped change the culture by making the idea of family planning OK starting in the '80s. I too could see myself innovating in Bangkok.

Bangkok was hot all year round. Bangkok was much cheaper than Tokyo. Bangkok was one of my favorite cities in the world. I wanted to live in Bangkok; I didn't want to work there. In fact, I didn't want to work in education anymore.

In one year, I'll turn forty. What did I want to be doing when I did? Definitely not working in a school. Traveling. Where? Where my lunch time and pee time weren't regulated by bells. To the Seventh Continent. Antarctica. How was I going to afford it? The "twenty dollars a day mindset" that I learned in 2006. Twenty dollars was the amount of money I felt I needed to live in Bangkok in 2006 when I quit my fancy job: Five to seven dollars a night for a dorm bed in a shared room and shared bath. Four to eight dollars a day for food and water. Three to seven for entertainment. About twenty dollars a day.

The twenty dollars a day mindset made me look at money differently. Half of the world then and today lives on one to two dollars a day. Traveling the world and building houses with sugarcane workers in Nicaragua, building a business with three sisters in El Salvador, and building a school with a phenomenal Panamanian woman in Bocas del Toro taught me that money gives choices, but it doesn't make you your highest and best self. It doesn't make you self-actualized.

Some people may say that my "twenty dollars a day mindset" made me a minimalist or frugal. It's true that I rarely buy anything that is new—my entire summer/spring wardrobe can fit in one blue Roughneck bin, and I prefer one-room living—but to me, this makes me intentional.

The twenty dollars a day mindset showed me how to live an intentional life that brings joy to me and those around me. It is grounded in three lessons that I learned living on twenty dollars a day; they guide me in life (and my business) no matter what my cash flow.

1. Interdependence. Take what you need. Give what you can. Your success is my success; my success is your success. It's stretching Stephen Covey's win-win into win-win-win. You win. I win. Collectively, our community wins.

I learned the importance of water in Nicaragua when I stood in line with María, the mother of the cinder block house I was building with Habitat for Humanity, to get drinkable water, only to be turned away after an hour of waiting. "*Suerte* [luck]!" they said. Better luck tomorrow. I stood in my privilege and ignorance and disbelief until María tugged at my hand, and we headed back to the build site. On this day, I understood the luxury of clean water.

I learned the power of perspective on Pentecost Island, Vanuatu. I went to the island to see the ceremonial land-diving for yams and ended up teaching the game "Red Light, Green Light" to first-graders. After teaching them "The Itsy Bitsy Spider" and "Little Bunny Foo Foo," we headed out to the field for a good old-fashioned game of "Red Light, Green Light." They were fast learners, so I was confused when they struggled with the concept that red means stop, green means go! They were confused too, so we both tried harder. And then I paused and reminded myself that I was on an island with no electricity and no cars; they had no reference to the significance of red and green. I laughed at my ignorance and taught the game from their eyes, not mine.

2. Choose good. In a country like the USA where bad sells, fear is our common denominator, and systemic inequity thrives, look for the good, trust in the good, and be the good in the world.

I learned the power of good when I had dengue in India and the housekeeper where I was staying understood what was wrong when my American friends did not. She woke me from my sleep during the day, made me eat broth, gave me rehydration salts, and watched to make sure I drank enough water before she would help me back to bed. She knew what to do and did it.

3. MOXIE. Have the guts, the grit, the energy, the pluck to do what you know needs to be done.

When I was in my twenties, my guy friends told me I would be a good entrepreneur. I replied, "That's crazy! I don't want to be the boss." But in my twenty years in education and my six years total of traveling around the world out of a backpack, the universal shrinking problem, from girls and women who live on one to two dollars a day in Bali to millionaires in Sydney, made me mad enough to do something that would make a bigger impact: start a business. I embraced my MOXIE and became the boss of my own business. My friends were right.

BACK IN THE USA, MAY 2014.

That one year turned into four years of living on twenty dollars a day. In addition to the three lessons, I learned how to re-purpose what I had in my medium-sized duffle bag. Shampoo worked to wash clothes. Duct tape was used instead of stitches on a remote island in Vanuatu. Floss was not only for your teeth but also a worthy clothesline when overlanding in Africa.

This is how I learned my efficient packing routine, the one I shared with my roommates in Puerto Rico years later: bring an outfit to interview in and a little black dress to party in, and choose a theme color so everything can be mixed and matched. Today, I still use this same concept. All my clothes are the same as my logo: hot pink, white, silver, and black. I've been told that I'm "on brand." But to me, it means I have fewer decisions to make and spend less money on stuff. And I can still fit everything I need for nine months of travel in a medium-sized duffle bag.

By living on twenty dollars a day, I was able to step away from materialism. From things. To really be present. To wait patiently and comfortably for the train, for a meal, for water. I no longer needed to hide behind things, job titles, or what others thought of me.

I still had privilege as an American, as a white woman, and as somebody who made enough money to have a savings account. It gave me freedom of time and place—the promise I made to myself when I quit my last job in Tokyo.

Living on twenty dollars a day takes MOXIE. Being a social entrepreneur takes MOXIE. Trying to live a self-actualized life takes MOXIE. If you did what you know you need to do, what would it be? MOXIE it.

HOW TO LIVE THE TWENTY DOLLARS A DAY MINDSET.

1. **Take up space.** American women control 85 percent of financial

decisions in a household[1]—your choices matter. A lot. Make sure each dollar you spend goes to where you want it. Being a feminist, I buy from women-owned businesses. Being a social entrepreneur, I buy from businesses that choose good and support a social mission. I buy gratitude gifts from The Giving Keys so that every necklace I buy supports job creation for people transitioning out of homelessness and upcycles a key.[2] I eat at All Square in Minneapolis, centered on craft grilled cheese and professional development for formerly incarcerated individuals.[3] I bank at Sunrise Banks, which is a socially responsible bank focused on creating financial empowerment for all; it is also a certified B corps business.[4] Your buying makes a big difference: for good or not. How will you be intentional about where you spend your money?

2. Be first. To model the twenty dollars a day mindset of interdependence when buying stuff. Try buying used. Consignment stores and thrift shops are great places to start. Patagonia (the outdoor gear store) is so focused on the interdependence between human consumption and the environment, they opened up Worn Wear, where you can buy used Patagonia gear and send in your used Patagonia gear to be sold or fixed, "because the best thing we can do for our planet is cut down on consumption and get more use out of stuff we already own."[5] How will you be intentional about your consumption and the environment?

3. Look for the helpers. You are not alone. Take what you need, give what you can. Win for you. Win for them. Win for the collective. What would a win-win-win intention give you?

NOW, GO BE INTENTIONAL.

1   Luscombe, Belina. "Woman Power: The Rise of the Sheconomy." *Time*. http://content.time.com/time/magazine/article/0,9171,2030913,00.html
2   https://www.thegivingkeys.com/
3   https://www.allsquarempls.com/
4   https://sunrisebanks.com/
5   https://wornwear.patagonia.com/

SPARKLE.

*The art of life is not controlling what happens
to us but using what happens to us.*

—GLORIA STEINEM

2019 WAS THE MOST PROFITABLE YEAR EVER.

So in January 2020 I chose SPARKLE as my word of the year
because it seemed fun and easy-peasy. In the beginning, I was
sparkling. I was experimenting with empathy, gender, and virtual reality; I was invited to be on a panel for UN Women at
SXSW on the subject of "The Power of Technology and Finance
for Women"; several Fortune 500 companies were curious about
the system-breaking work I was doing around Men as Change
Agents; I was scheduled to showcase *Quit Being So Good* for
International Women's Day; I had booked a month in Bali for
my annual MEtreat; and I had four speaking engagements confirmed for when I returned. "Sparkle on, Kristi. Sparkle on," I
said to myself.

And then COVID-19 struck. The first domino to fall was
SXSW. Then the speaking engagements. Next was Bali. And
then, it was quiet.

I have faced failure before. I flipped my life upside down before. I could do this. I would be OK. And heck, maybe even a
better human than before.

DECEMBER 2006.

In my first year of living on twenty dollars a day—after quitting my horrible-boss job and before my four-year journey—I wrote a book about *being*. My goal every day was to just BE (and stay within my twenty-dollars-a-day budget).

I went from a suit-wearing, important-decision-making, school-running principal to a bucket-carrying, dorm-sharing, sweaty janitor mopping up eighteen-year-olds' used condoms. It was Fiji's South Sea Islands' fault.

Mana Island in Fiji was too tempting. The sea cucumbers called to me, "*Kristi, come snorkel. Kayak our tiny island. Don't miss the beauty as you focus on your budget.*" The sea cucumbers were wise and a bit impulsive.

At a hostel in Brisbane, Australia, I was journaling and working on my budget in the lobby waiting for my bed to be ready in an all-women four-bunk room with en suite. My twenty dollars a day budget came to six hundred dollars a month.

It was the second month of my seven-month adventure, and the sea cucumbers and I spent a hundred dollars on a day in Fiji.

This was more than a problem; it felt like a failure. Self-doubt invaded. *What if I run out of money? What if I fail at traveling too?*

I noticed I was holding my breath. Pause. I took a deep warrior-pose breath. I would figure this out; I always did.

Eerily, a godly voice came from the loudspeaker above: "G'day, mates. We are in need of somebody to clean rooms for a free night of accommodation and a pitcher of beer." By staying three nights for free and eating one meal a day, I would be able to recover from Fiji and keep traveling. I leapt from my seat and was the first to the counter to claim the job. *I figured it out.*

At 10:00 a.m., I showed up to help Linda, the head of house-cleaning, clean the fifty community rooms. Linda was an un-assuming, efficient machine; her energy was kind and industri-ous and her smile contagious. Her glasses were spotted from her work, and her ponytail was pulled tight, which showed her smile off more.

As a proper cleaning lady, I was to change the rubbish bags and mop the bathroom floors. These are two of my least favorite tasks. When I worked at Burger King in high school, I avoided them as much as possible. Twenty years later, I was face to face with it. For two hours. Three days in a row.

In reality, I avoided all domestic work. Growing up in a very traditional home where my allowance of two dollars a week was based on me doing the dishes every night and cleaning the bath-room weekly, while my brother's only job for the same allow-ance was to take out the garbage once a week (which my mom often did anyway), I understood gender inequity young.

As I watched my mom scramble to take care of three chil-dren, make sure the house was spick and span when my dad walked in the door, and cook for us all, I made one of my Life's Declarations: "Nobody will marry me because I cook and clean." Now, at thirty-six, I was single and traveling the world out of a backpack. Other than worrying an itty-bitty bit about money, I was a free bird.

I embraced the opportunity, put on gloves, filled the yellow commercial bucket with pink gunk, and confided in Linda that for the past six years, I had hired a cleaning lady. I had my house cleaned by somebody who liked cleaning and at the same time supported a woman business owner. Win-win-win! Linda gig-gled appreciatively at the irony and handed me the drippy, dirty, dingy mop.

Each of the fifty rooms had its own bathroom and shower and at least four backpackers. The first room's resident had left a trail of last night's escapades: McDonald's wrappers, soiled underwear, empty beer bottles, and a used condom stuck to the floor. Quickly, I mopped it under the bed and picked up the garbage bin to appear busy. Gloves or not, I did not intend on picking up that.

I followed Linda to the next room: an all-male eight-bed dorm room. I knew from experience that nothing good happens when you get eight men together. Read the news. The garbage was overflowing, five were sleeping off a hangover, and the odor of flatulence and recycled alcohol permeated the room. I avoided making eye contact with any of the residents strewn out in their beds.

The shower reeked of vomit, and my mop slopped over the feasting cockroaches that ran wildly into cracks and crevices away from my mop. *This way I don't have to kill them,* I thought. I don't kill bugs. Exception: mosquitos. Mosquitos can kill you with dengue; I knew this from personal experience with that illness in Delhi. I hadn't died (obviously), but at one point I was delirious enough from high fevers to not care so much about living.

Hungover moans greeted us from the next room. Frightened, I backed away from the door, but Linda forged through and started cleaning. One of the boys turned around in bed and opened his mouth. A putrid smell filled the room. I gagged.

Is this really worth twenty dollars? Maybe this was a time to take out my credit card. It felt like an emergency. I thought of all the other disgusting things I had done as a backpacker, and this wasn't the worst. I had toileted with a tapeworm, which at the time I wasn't sure came from me or from the sewer system. I'd flicked furry creatures off my body on a soiled mattress infested with bedbugs. I'd survived dengue.

Linda unlocked the room at the end of the hall and warned, "This room is bad." *What were the other rooms?* I wondered. I stuck a toe in, looked both ways, and entered. Two were sleeping, one was doing something that is meant for private time, and one boy closest to the shower eyed me sheepishly. The way his eyes twittered, his face jerked, and his smile spread sent chills up my spine. He was checking me out, which proved it doesn't matter what we women wear—we are objectified. I was wearing plastic gloves and a baseball cap to keep my hair from getting dirty from the mop, sweating profusely, and ripe with the nastiness of the day.

Trying not to trip over his expensive camera, Union Jack flip-flops, wet socks, and gray briefs, I tramped my way to the shower. He followed me with his eyes. If I had met him on an empty street at night, I would not have been safe. His look was more than the occasional "flirtatious" looks, which are also not welcome but not dangerous. Usually. I was the cleaning lady, not a prospect.

Lost in thought and disgusted at being objectified by Union Jack, I lost my footing in the wet droppings of the mop. I flapped my arms wildly to avoid crashing onto the unforgiving concrete floor or worse yet, his bed. I regained balance and stomped into the shower. I sloshed the mop around the corners of the tiled shower stall, cursed my old age (thirty-six) under my breath, and gingerly stepped out of the shower stall. I was face to face with Union Jack.

A standoff. Who was going to move out of the way? I'd be damned if it was me. I had my master's, had worked longer than he'd been alive, and was an American woman and a FEMINIST. I lifted my slimy mop and dangled it in front of me. Full of the filth of the morning rounds, it dripped a puddle between us. He understood; I was not afraid to use it. He slid to the side, and I sauntered past. Carefully—I wouldn't want to fall.

Feeling victorious, I glanced at my watch. 12:28 p.m. Free bird! I bid Linda farewell, took the stairs two at a time to my room on the fourth floor, gathered up my laptop, and headed to the bathroom before my trek downtown for my iced coffee reward.

While sitting on the toilet, I glanced down and couldn't help but notice how clean and shiny the floor was. The floor I had cleaned. I could almost see my reflection smiling back at me. *I will be OK,* I thought.

JANUARY 2021.

Even though life moves fast, it may feel slow and not so sparkly. In these times, dig deeper than confidence. To me, confidence is dependent on affirmations from others or your own self-talk. Step into self-assurance. Self-assurance is that place where even when you are put on an "Action Plan," are rejected by someone you thought would be there forever, and spend more money than you make, you believe, "I will figure it out. I will be OK."

Go ahead. Say it out loud. "I will figure it out. I will be OK." Breathe it in. Trust in it. Believe it.

Breathe it out. "I will figure it out. I will be OK." That is self-assurance.

HOW TO PRACTICE SELF-ASSURANCE.

1. **Take up space.** Self-assurance: believing you will be OK. Even if you fail. Even if you run out of money. Even if a pandemic takes over the world. Knowing you'll be OK is probably the biggest way to take up space because when you believe in your highest and best self, you will live your life to the fullest. When things don't go how you want them to, pause—it's a moment. Not a life. What would believing "I will be OK" give you?

2. **Be first.** Jump at the chance to clean rooms in exchange for a free room and a pitcher of beer! Be the first to see the opportunity in the mundane. Be the first to do the unexpected. Follow your gut, not your head. Be the first to save yourself and be your own happy ending. What challenge is an opportunity waiting for you?

3. **Look for the helpers.** I've had lots of helpers. Some I know, like my high school Guns N' Roses–listening friend Mark, who

gave me the chance to disrupt the power systems in corporate America. Some are strangers, like the woman in Nicaragua who intervened when I was being harassed on the bus at the risk of being targeted herself. But the ultimate helper is me. I believe in myself enough to pay myself each month for working toward what matters to me the most—a safe and equitable world for women. I continue to create a life built on freedom of time and place. And I am intentional on where and who I spend my headspace and heartspace on. How will you help yourself?

RIGHT NOW, BE YOUR OWN HAPPY ENDING.

THANK YOU, GLORIA STEINEM.

*A feminist is anyone who recognizes the equality
and full humanity of women and men.*

—GLORIA STEINEM

MINNEAPOLIS, 2014.

I was at a high school, about to meet with a group of young women who were interested in my Changemakers Course. There was a freshman boy sitting there as I set up, and he asked what I was doing. When I turned to tell him, his teacher chimed in, "She's doing feminist work."

The student looked at him and asked, "What's a feminist?"

His teacher replied, "I'm a feminist. Are you a feminist?"

Looking lost and confused, he said, "I don't know."

He replied, "Look it up."

I was anxious. I wanted so badly to share Hillary Clinton's quote, "Human rights are women's rights, and women's rights are human rights"; to defend feminism; to tell him that it wasn't an F word. But I followed his teacher's lead, even though I was fearful he'd find the Urban Dictionary definition: *A woman who turns a relationship with a bad father or husband into a political agenda, seeking not equality, but revenge.*

The boy went to the Almighty Google, and read it out loud, slowly. "The belief that women should be allowed the same rights, power, and opportunities as men and be treated in the same way."

His teacher asked, "So, are you a feminist?"

I was a feminist when I called myself a feminist.

I was a feminist every time I rejected the "Quit Being So Good" message the world was telling me.

I was a feminist when I was told by my professor that women couldn't stand up in front of large groups and lead, so I co-created and co-led the Challenge of Teaching Conference at my university.

I was a feminist when, as a teacher, I created a safe space for girls to fail and boys to cry in my classroom.

I was a feminist when I gobbled up authors like Gloria Steinem, Maya Angelou, Sylvia Plath, Amy Tan, and Zora Neale Hurston.

I was a feminist when, as an intern at the Houston Area Women's Center, I co-created and co-led a group of men focusing on the healing of their own sexual abuse growing up and rehabilitation from domestic violence.

I was a feminist when I was almost fired for allowing the group to choose the topic of LGBTQ at my SEED (Seeking Educational Equity and Diversity) meeting.

I was a feminist when I founded Academy for Women's Empowerment to create a safer and more equitable world for women.

I was a feminist when I marched with other women at the first Women's March in January 2017.

I was a feminist when I wrote and published *Quit Being So Good* to inspire changemakers to disrupt the systems of power and create a more equitable and safer world for women.

His teacher asked, "So, are you a feminist?"

He paused. Scanned his screen, looked up, and said, "Yeah. I guess I am."

And you can be one too.

HOW TO BE A FEMINIST.

1. **Take up space.** For women and girls. For men and boys. To me, being a feminist is expecting, demanding, and fighting for "the equality and full humanity of women AND men." In The Representation Project's documentary "The Mask You Live In," it is said that the three most destructive words you can say to a boy is "Be a man." As an educator and businesswoman who has worked with boys and men, I see and feel their pain as limits are forced on their identity too. How will you be aware of stereotypes and limiting beliefs that limit boys/men as well as girl/ women?

2. **Be first.** To call yourself a feminist. "If you say, I'm for equal pay, that's a reform. If you say, I'm a feminist, that's a transformation of society," said Gloria. How will you transform society? Start small. Look right in front of you. What needs to be changed to create a more equal world for all? That's where you start. What is your first step?

3. **Look for the helpers.** Look beyond gender. Find partnerships in the intersectionality of "full humanity." Some of my favorite "helpers" are SEED (Seeking Educational Equity and Diversity), founded by Peggy McIntosh (author of "White Privilege: Unpacking Your Invisible Backpack"), Family Tree Clinic in Minnesota, and Project Diva International. Who are your partners?

GO FORTH, FULL HUMAN. MOXIEon!

Gratitudes

TO MY DREAM KEEPERS.

This is what fifty looks like.

—KRISTI HEMMER

Writing and publishing *Quit Being So Good* has been my dream since I was eight; thank you for being part of the dream. Gratitudes to my Dream Keepers, who have protected my dream of being a published author from, as Langston Hughes wrote, "the too-rough fingers of the world" all along.

Linda Hemmer: for believing that I was always writing a book.

Dennis Hemmer: for teaching me not to give up.

Michael Bartus: for loving me as a single, childless woman.

Amy Quale: for believing the three steps could dismantle the patriarchy.

A-team: for encouraging me to write the book and believing that it was a Big Deal.

Team Kristi: for the feedback, the pushback, and the "I have your back."

My students (young and old and the young who are now old): for making me a better human.

My teachers (like Mrs. Cain, Mrs. Boyes, and Mrs. Leifker): who inspired me to teach, to write, and to love unconditionally.

Maya Angelou's *I Know Why the Caged Bird Sings*: for making me not feel so alone.

Gloria Steinem's *Revolution from Within*: for "getting" me.

Mary Pipher's *Reviving Ophelia*: for inspiring me to own my power and make sure other girls and women do too.

The Wise Ink team: for your extra hours, love, and time for making my voice readable.

You, the Reader: for your trust and guts in reading until the MOXIE end.

IN LOVE AND MOXIE,

Kristi

About the Author

Kristi, age eight, when she first declared she was going to be an author.

Why do women and girls shrink in a classroom, boardroom, and conversation? This question made educator Kristi Hemmer so mad that she quit her six-figure job in Tokyo to answer the question and solve the problem. For four years, she traveled the world on twenty dollars a day learning about social entrepreneurship. In the process, she founded Academy for Women's Empowerment (AWE). AWE has inspired thousands of changemakers around the world to disrupt the systems of power and create a safer and more equitable for women and girls. Kristi Hemmer has a master's degree in education. She lives in Minneapolis, Minnesota, and everywhere else in the world, for that matter. To learn more or invite Kristi to your organization, visit www.kristihemmer.com.